RECORDED VERSIONS
GUITAR

AUTHENTIC TRANSCRIPTIONS
WITH NOTES AND TABLATURE

RED HOT CHILI PEPPERS GREATEST HITS

ISBN 0-634-07390-7

HAL•LEONARD®
CORPORATION

7777 W. BLEUMOUND RD. P.O. BOX 13819 MILWAUKEE, WI 53213

Visit Hal Leonard Online at
www.halleonard.com

Under the Bridge

Words and Music by Anthony Kiedis, Flea, John Frusciante and Chad Smith

* Symbols in parenthesis represent chord names respective to
capoed guitar. Symbols above reflect actual sounding chord,
and overall tonality.

1. Some-times I feel ___ like I don't have a part-ner. Some-times I feel ___ like

Give It Away

Words and Music by Anthony Kiedis, Flea, John Frusciante and Chad Smith

Gtr. 1: w/ Riff A, 1 1/2 times, simile

What I've got, you've got to get it, put it in you.
Low brow, but I rock a lit - tle know how.

What I've got, you've got to get it, put it in you.
Get smart, get down with the pow - er,

Reel - ing with the feel - ing, don't stop, con - tin - ue.
nev - er been a bet - ter time than right now.

Re - a - lize ___ I don't wan - na be a mi - ser,
Bob Mar - ley, po - et and a proph - et,

con - fide with Sly, you'll be the wi - ser.
Bob Mar - ley taught me how to off it.

To Coda 1 ⊕

To Coda 2 ⊕

Young blood is the lov - in' up - ri - ser.
Bob Mar - ley walk - in' like he talk it.

How come ev - 'ry - bod - y wan - na keep it like the Kai - ser?
Good - ness me, can't you see I'm gon - na cough it?

Gtr. 1

1/4

1/4

Chorus

N.C.(A5)

Give it a - way, give it a - way, give it a - way now. ___
Give it a - way, give it a - way, give it a - way now. ___

*Two gtrs. arr. for one.

1/2

1.

Give it a - way, give it a - way, give it a - way now. ___ I can't tell if I'm a king - pin or a pau - per!

full   full   full

⊕ *Coda 2*
Out-Chorus

Give it a-way, give it a-way, give it a-way now. Give it a-way, give it a-way, give it a-way, now.

Give it a-way, give it a-way, give it a-way now. Give it a-way, give it a-way, give it a-way, now.

Give it a-way now. Give it a-way now.

w/ Voc. Fig. 1, 18 times

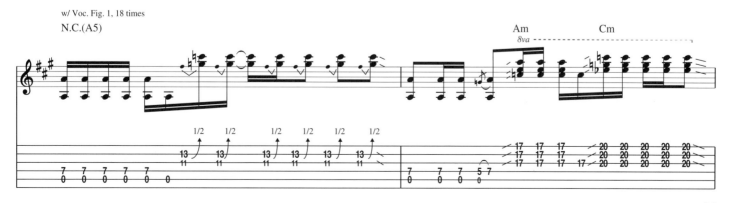

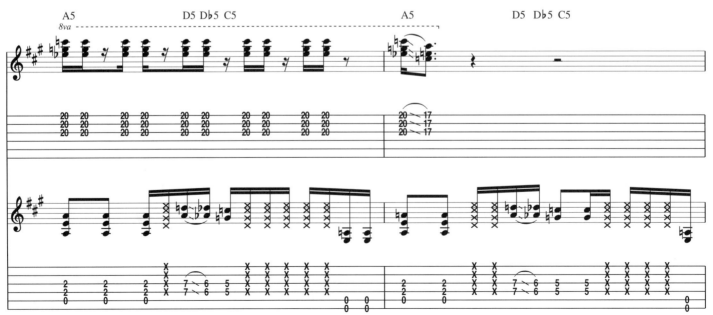

Additional Lyrics

3. Lucky me, swimmin' in my ability,
Dancin' down on life with agility.
Come and drink it up from my fertility,
Blessed with a bucket of lucky mobility.

My mom, I love her 'cause she love me,
Long gone are the times when she scrub me.
Feelin' good, my brother gonna hug me,
Drink up my juice, young love, chug-a-lug me.

There's a river born to be a giver,
Keep you warm, won't let you shiver.
His heart is never gonna wither,
Come on everybody, time to deliver.

Californication

Words and Music by Anthony Kiedis, Flea, John Frusciante and Chad Smith

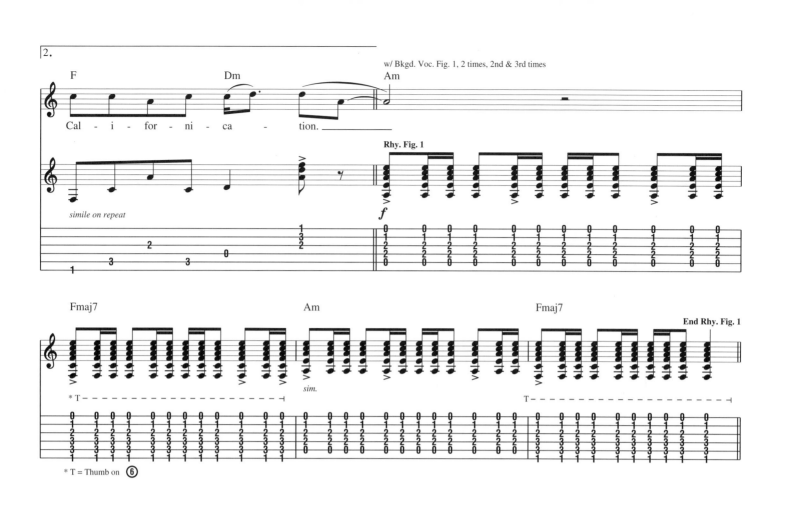

Pre-Chorus

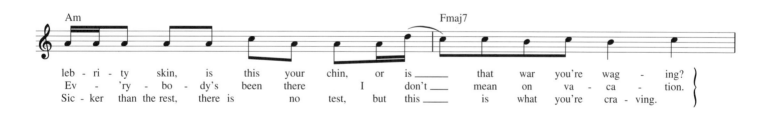

Pay your sur-geon ver-y well to break __ the spell of a - ging. __ Ce -
Born and raised by those __ who praise, con - trol of pop - u - la - tion. __
Pay your sur-geon ver-y well to break __ the spell of a - ging. __

leb - ri - ty skin, is this your chin, or is _____ that war you're wag - ing?
Ev - 'ry - bo - dy's been there I don't __ mean on va - ca - tion.
Sic - ker than the rest, there is no test, but this _____ is what you're cra - ving.

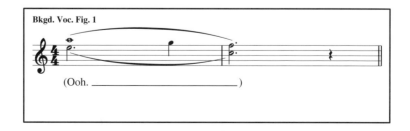

First born un - i - corn, _____ hard - core __ soft porn. _____

(Ooh. _____)

Chorus

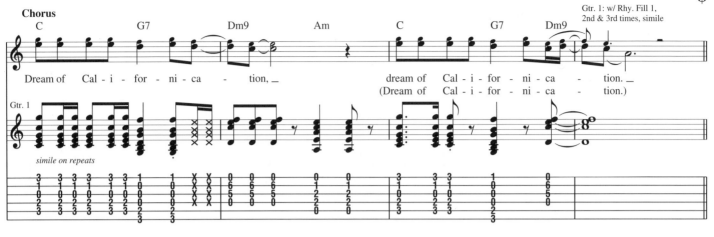

Interlude

D.S. al Coda 1
(take repeat)

Gtr. 1: w/ Riff A, 2 times

Coda 1

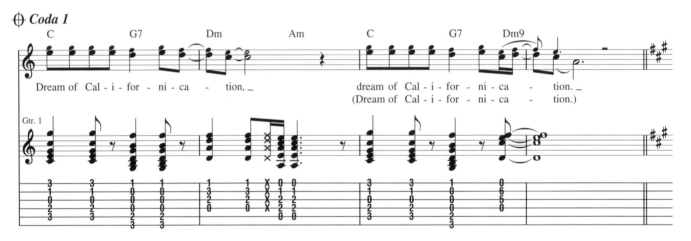

Guitar Solo

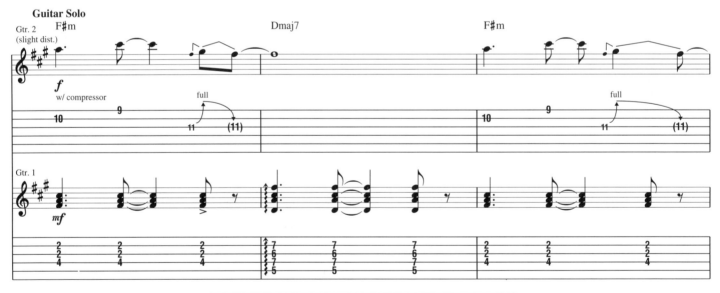

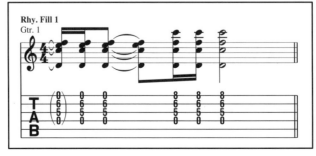

* Slight vibrato throughout.

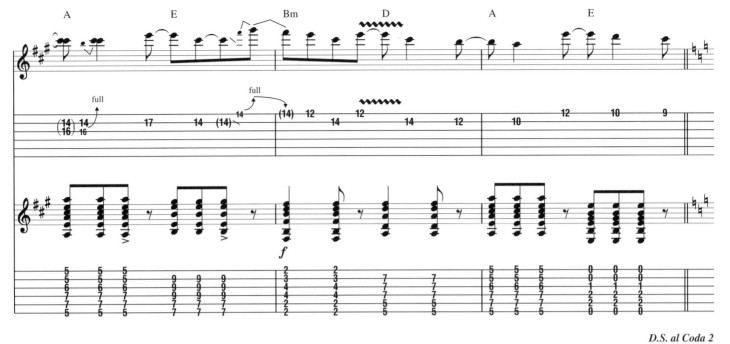

D.S. al Coda 2
(take 2nd ending)

Gtr. 1: w/ Riff A, 2 times

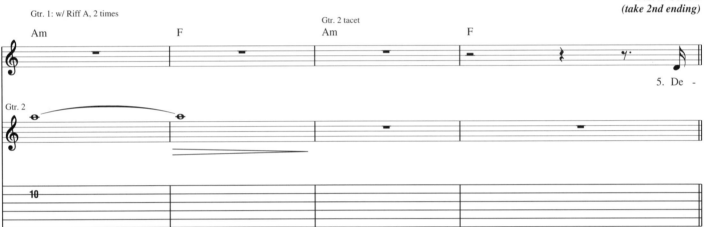

5. De -

⊕ *Coda 2*

Dream of Cal - i - for - ni - ca - tion, _____ dream of Cal - i - for - ni - ca - tion.
(Dream of Cal - i - for - ni - ca - tion.)

Additional Lyrics

4. Space may be the final frontier,
But it's made in a Hollywood basement;
Cobain can you hear the spheres
Singing songs off station to station.
And Alderon's not far away;
It's Californication.

5. Destruction leads to a very rough road
But it also breeds creation;
And earthquakes are to a girl's guitar,
They're just another good vibration
And tidal waves couldn't save the world
From Californication.

18

Scar Tissue

Words and Music by Anthony Kiedis, Flea, John Frusciante and Chad Smith

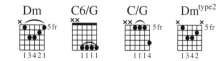

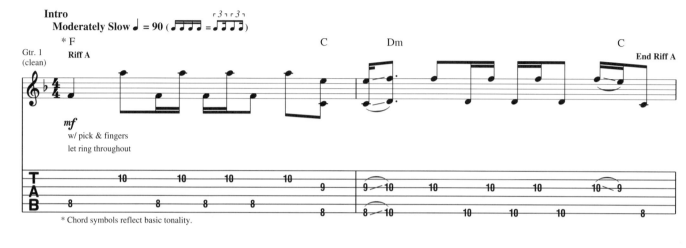

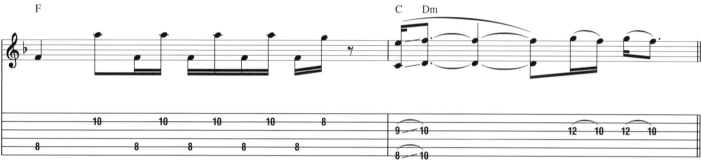

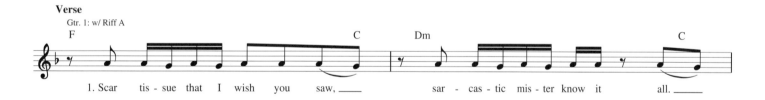

Guitar Solo

Verse

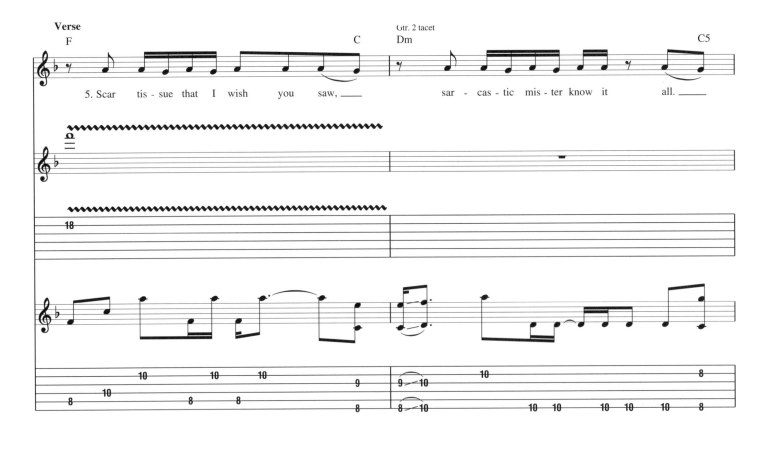

5. Scar tis-sue that I wish you saw, ___ sar - cas - tic mis - ter know it all. ___

Ah, close your eyes and I'll ___ kiss you 'cause ___ with the birds I'll share, ___

Chorus

with the birds I'll share this lone - ly ___ view, ___ with the birds I'll share this lone -
(I will share ___ this lone - ly... I will share ___ this lone -

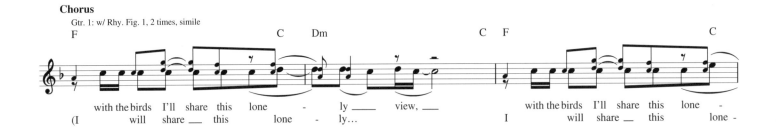

- ly ___ view, ___ with the birds I'll share this lone - ly view. ____
- ly... I will share ___ this lone ly...)

Outro-Guitar Solo

Soul to Squeeze

from the Paramount Motion Picture THE CONEHEADS

Words and Music by Anthony Kiedis, Flea, John Frusciante and Chad Smith

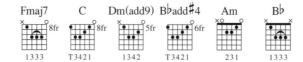

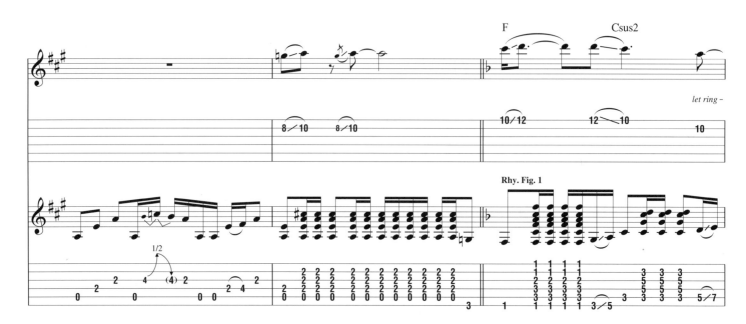

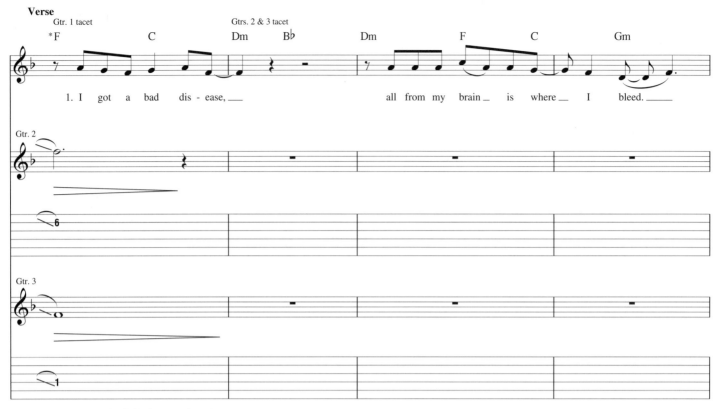

*Chord symbols implied by bass (next 8 meas.)

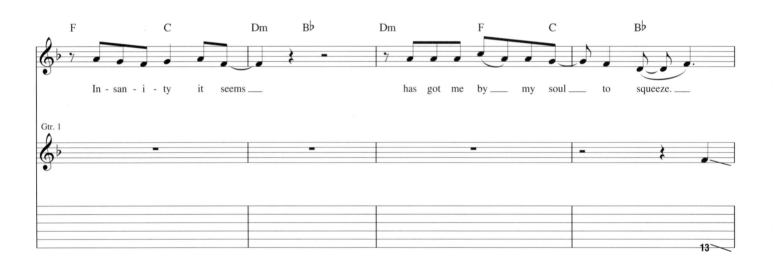

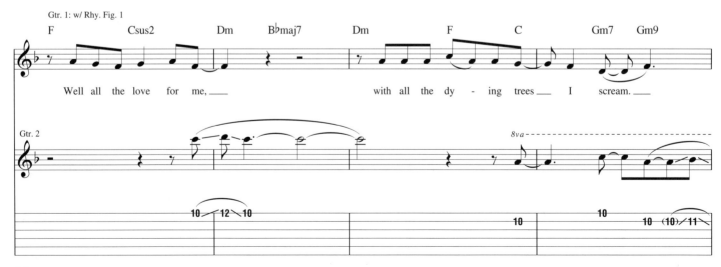

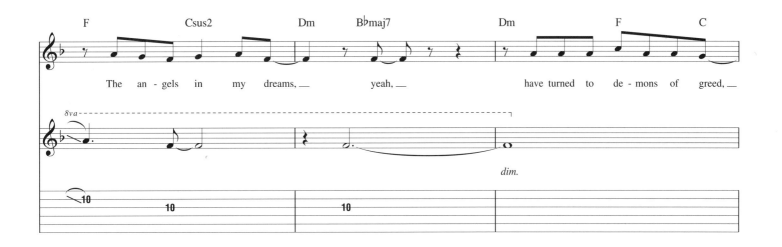

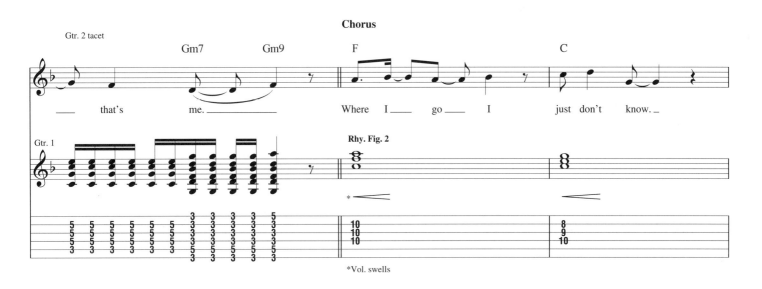

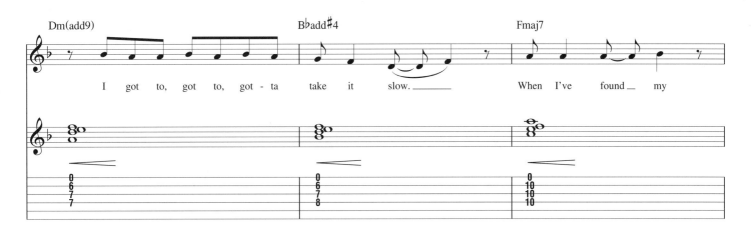

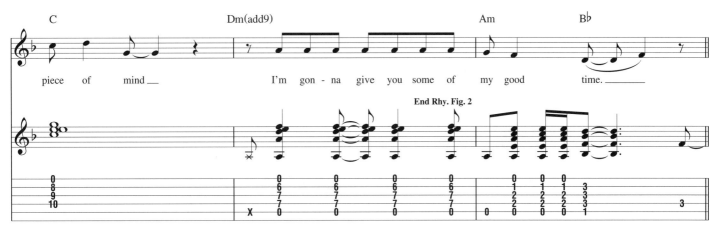

Verse

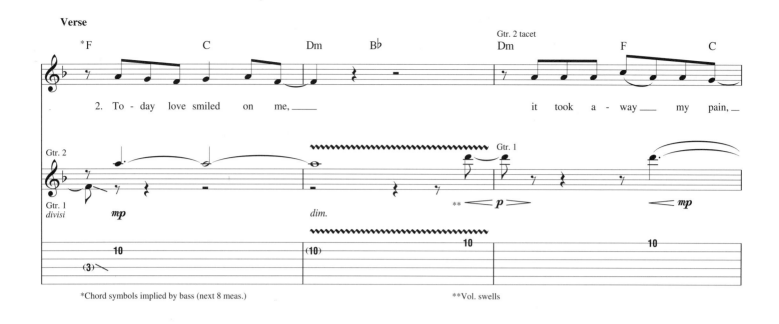

*Chord symbols implied by bass (next 8 meas.)   **Vol. swells

Chorus

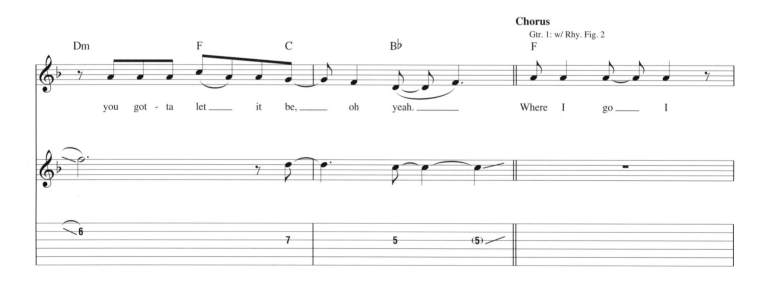

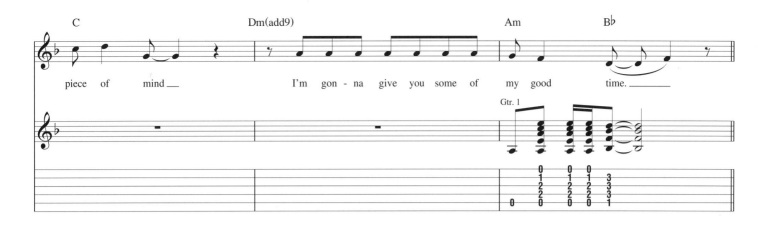

piece of mind ___ I'm gon - na give you some of my good time. ___

Guitar Solo

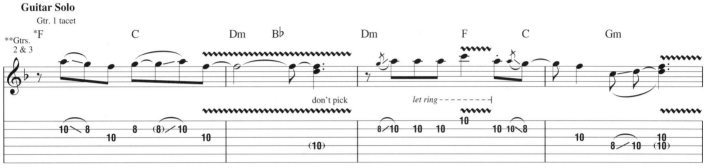

*Chord symbols implied by bass (next 8 meas.)
**Composite arrangement

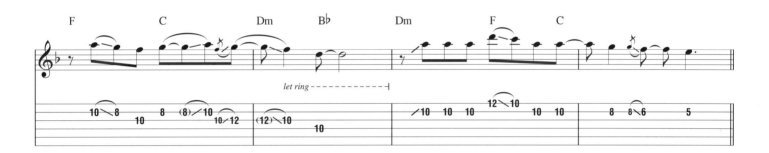

Interlude

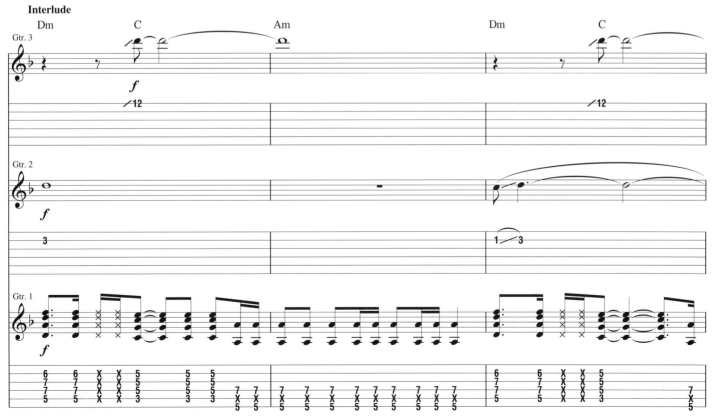

Verse

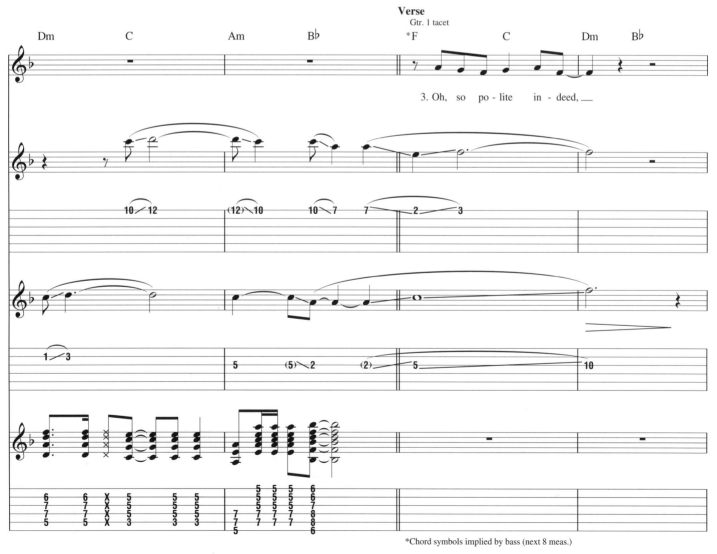

*Chord symbols implied by bass (next 8 meas.)

Otherside

Words and Music by Anthony Kiedis, Flea, John Frusciante and Chad Smith

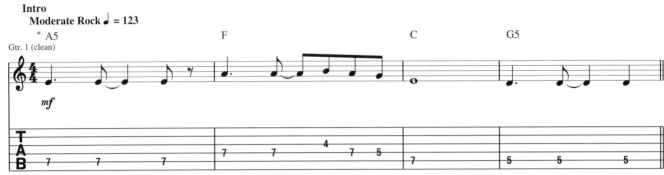

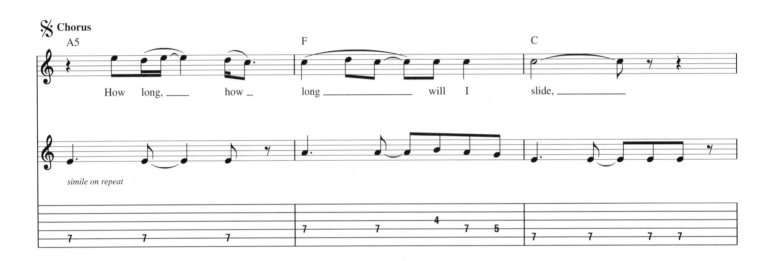

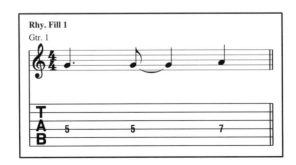

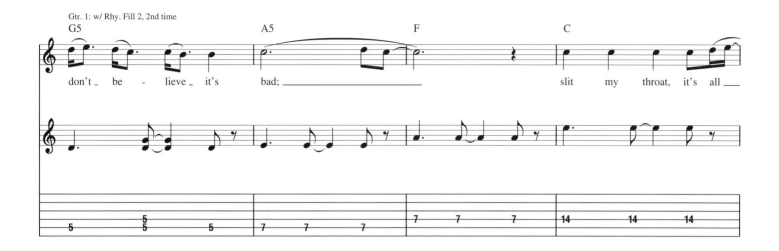

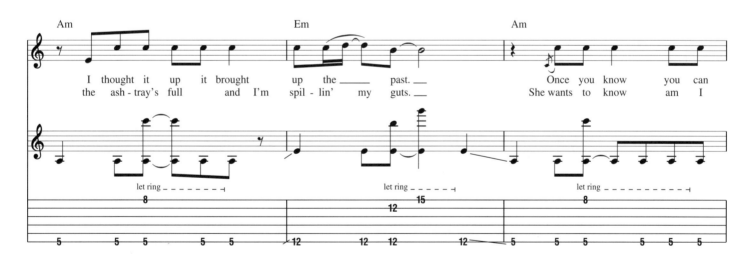

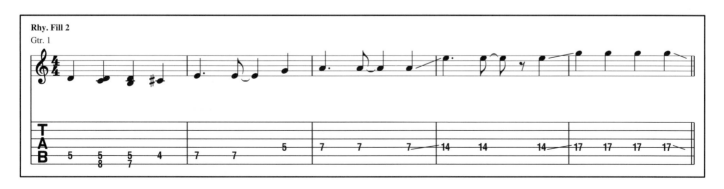

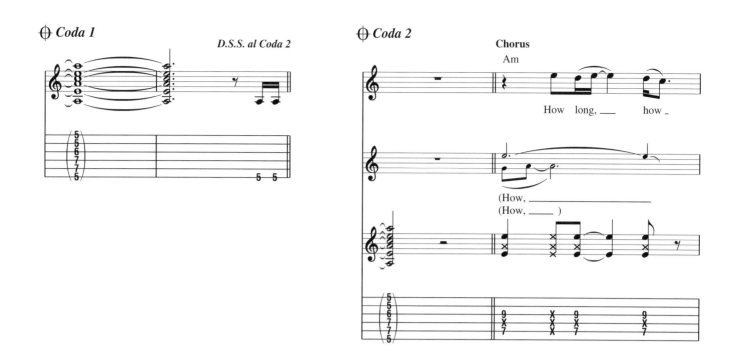

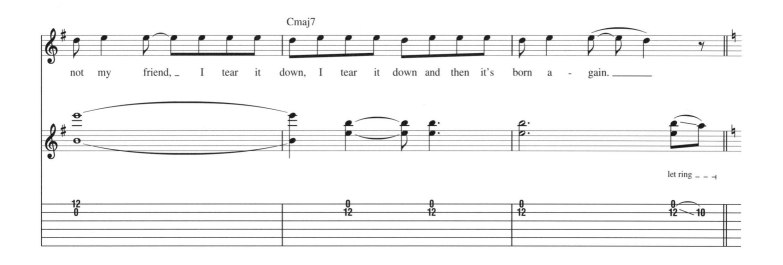

not my friend, _ I tear it down, I tear it down and then it's born a - gain. _____

let ring _ _ _

Guitar Solo

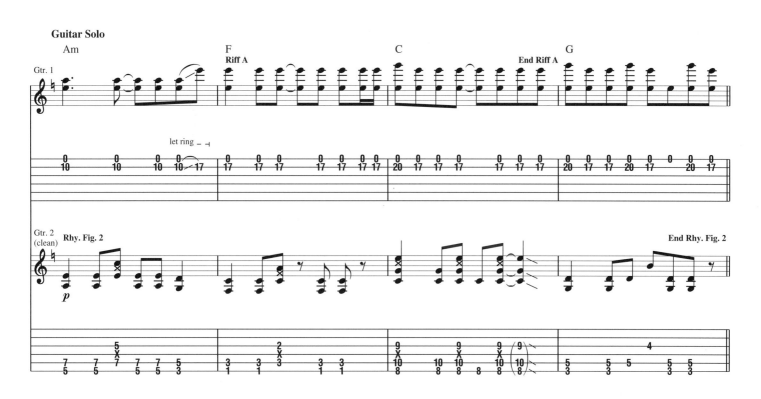

let ring _ _

Outro-Chorus

Gtr. 2: w/ Rhy. Fig. 2, 4 3/4 times, simile
** Gtr. 1: w/ Riff A, 8 times, simile

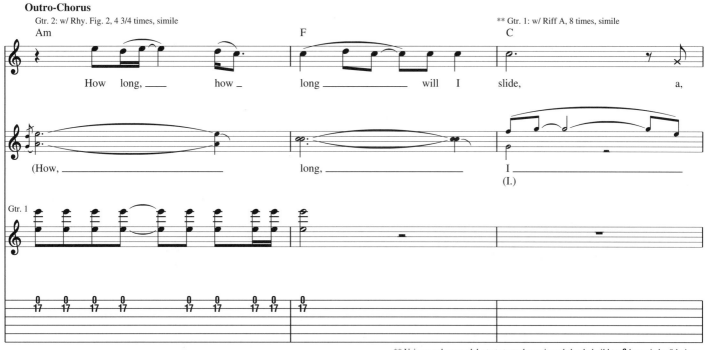

How long, ____ how _ long ____ will I slide, a,

(How, _____ long, _____ I
(I.)

** Using a volume pedal, start at **pp** dynamic and slowly build to **f** dynamic by 8th time.

Suck My Kiss

Words and Music by Anthony Kiedis, Flea, John Frusciante and Chad Smith

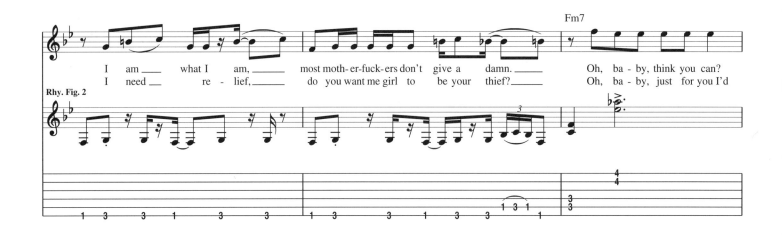

I am ___ what I am, ___ most moth-er-fuck-ers don't give a damn. ___ Oh, ba-by, think you can?
I need ___ re-lief, ___ do you want me girl to be your thief? ___ Oh, ba-by, just for you I'd

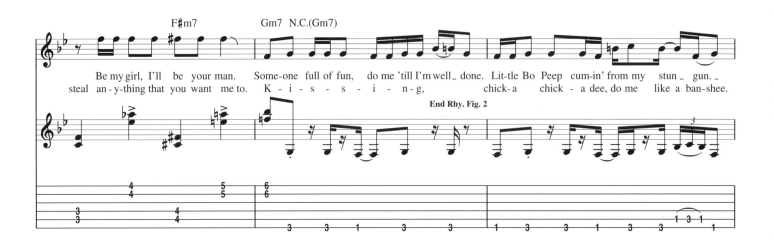

Be my girl, I'll be your man. Some-one full of fun, do me 'till I'm well_ done. Lit-tle Bo Peep cum-in' from my stun_ gun. _
steal an-y-thing that you want me to. K - i - s - s - i - n - g, chick-a chick-a dee, do me like a ban-shee.

Be - ware, ___ take care, ___ most moth-er fuck-ers have a cold-ass stare. ___
Low brow, ___ is how, ___ swim-ming in the sound of bow wow wow. ___

Oh, ba-by, please be there, suck my kiss, cut me my share. ___
Oh, ba-by, do me now, do me here I do al - low. ___

Chorus

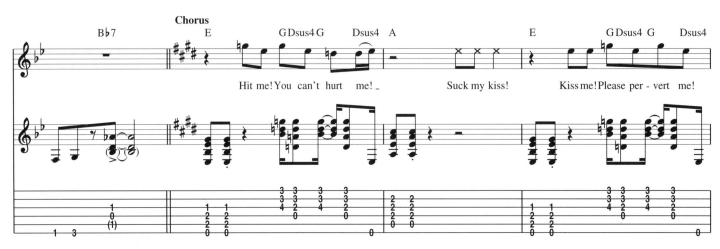

Hit me! You can't hurt me! _ Suck my kiss! Kiss me! Please per - vert me!

44

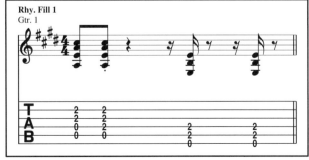

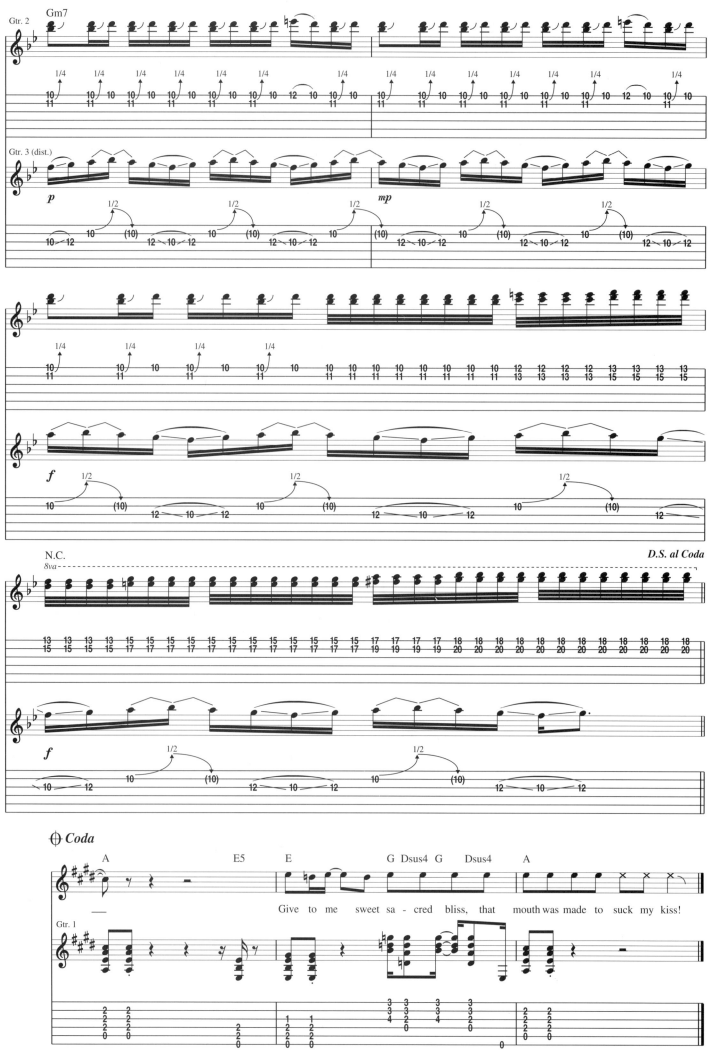

D.S. al Coda

Coda

Give to me sweet sa - cred bliss, that mouth was made to suck my kiss!

By the Way

Words and Music by Anthony Kiedis, Flea, John Frusciante and Chad Smith

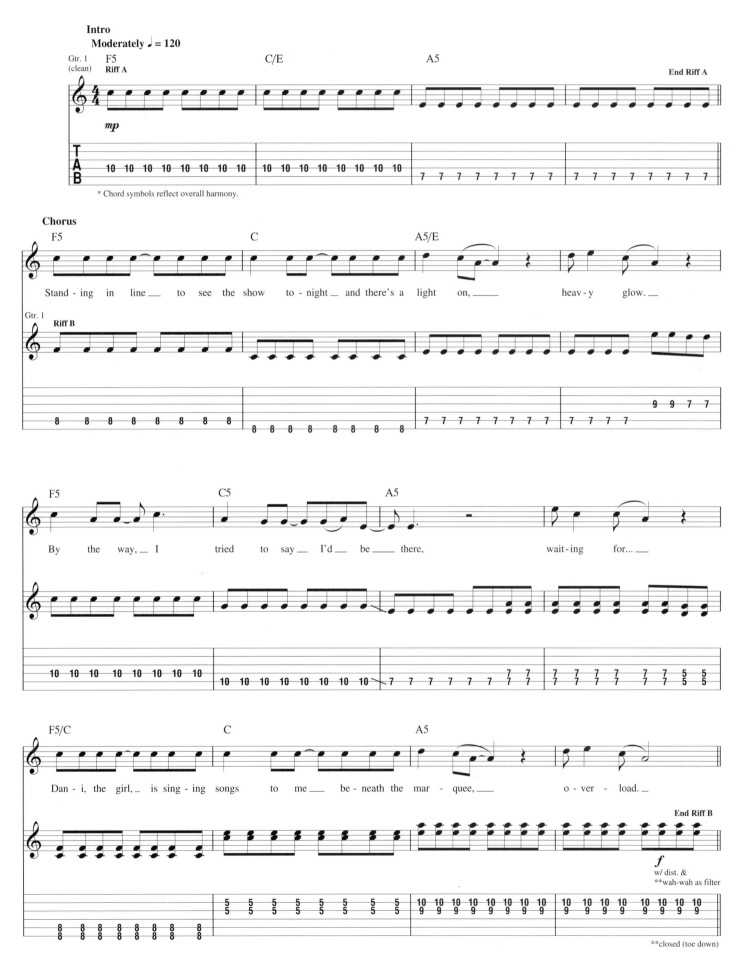

* Chord symbols reflect overall harmony.

** closed (toe down)

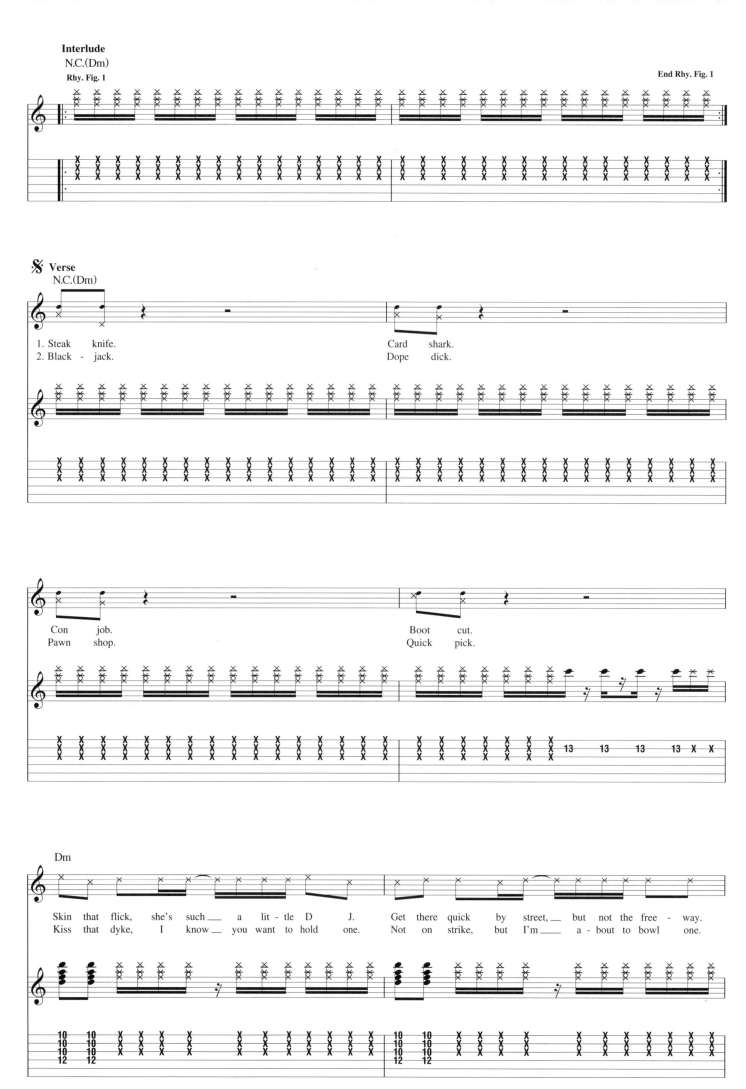

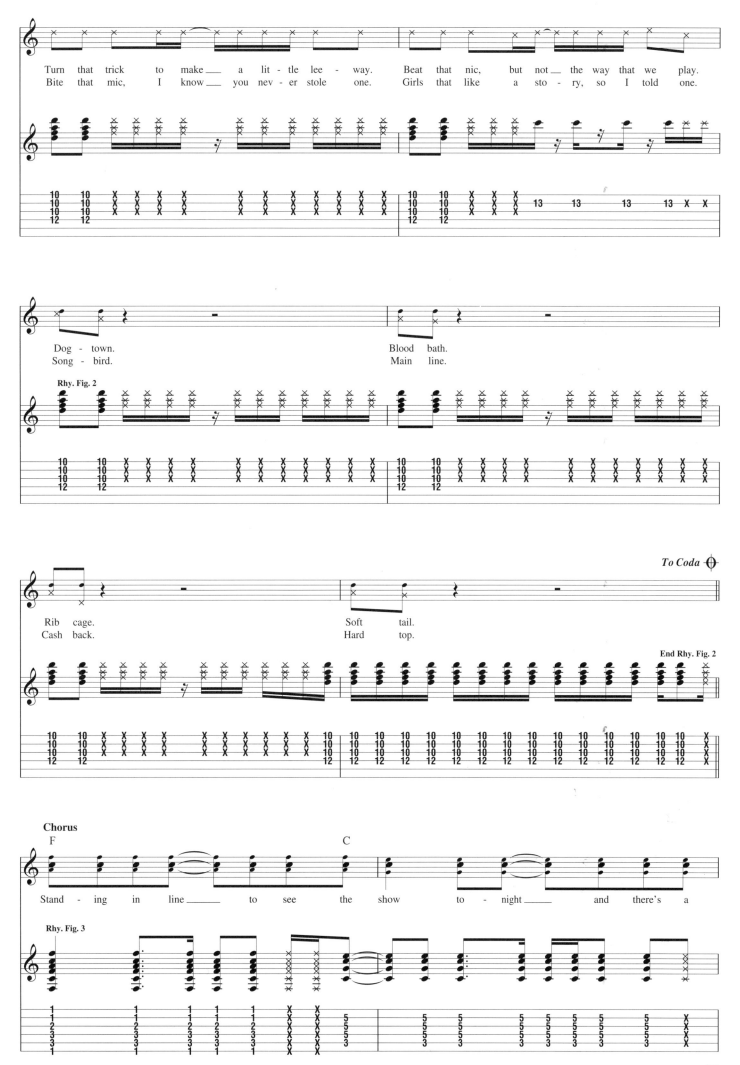

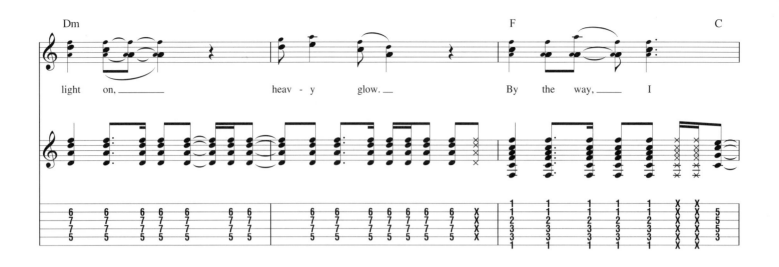

light on, _____ heav - y glow. _____ By the way, _____ I

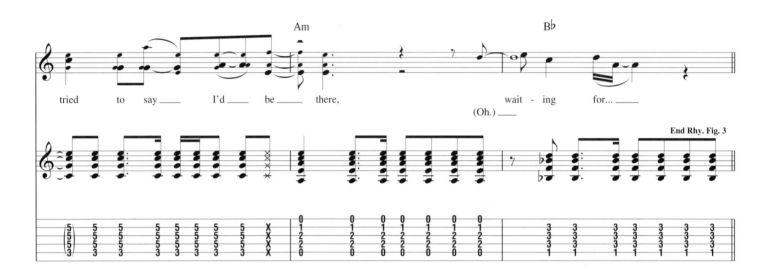

tried to say _____ I'd _____ be _____ there, wait - ing for... _____
(Oh.) _____

End Rhy. Fig. 3

Interlude
Gtr. 1: w/ Rhy. Fig. 1 (2 times)

D.S. al Coda

N.C.(Dm)

Vocoder

Coda
Chorus
Gtr. 1: w/ Riff A

F5   C/E   A5

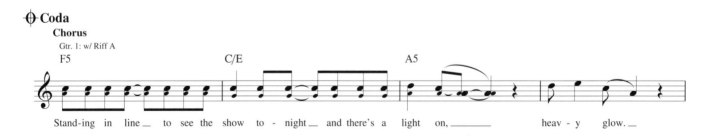

Stand-ing in line _____ to see the show to - night _____ and there's a light on, _____ heav - y glow. _____

Gtr. 1: w/ Riff B

F5   C5   A5/E

By the way, _____ I tried to say _____ I'd be _____ there, wait - ing for... _____

Dan - i, the girl, __ is sing - ing songs to me __ be - neath the mar - quee, _____ o - ver - sold. __

By the way, __ I tried to say __ I'd be __ there, wait - ing for... _____

Interlude

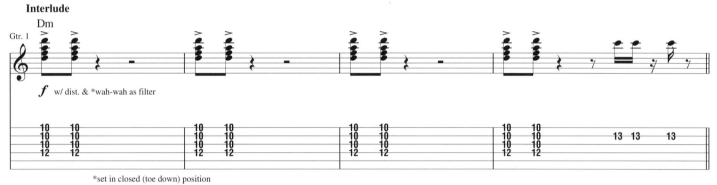

*w/ dist. & *wah-wah as filter*

*set in closed (toe down) position

Bridge

w/ Voc. ad lib (next 8 meas.)

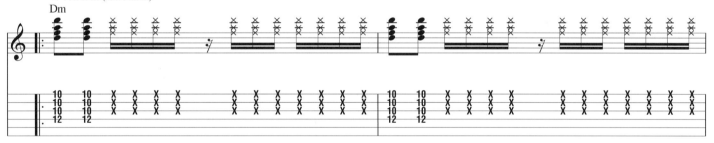

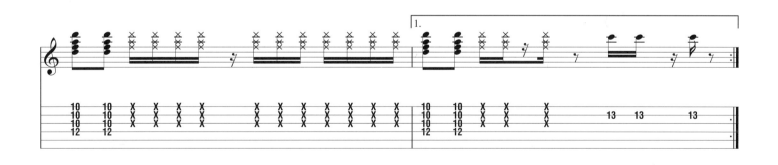

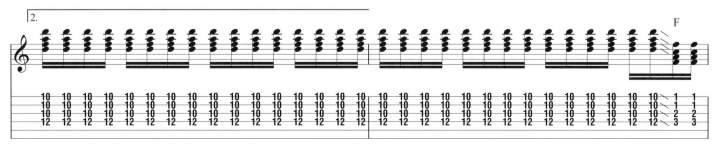

Chorus

Gtr. 1: w/ Rhy. Fig. 3 (2 times)

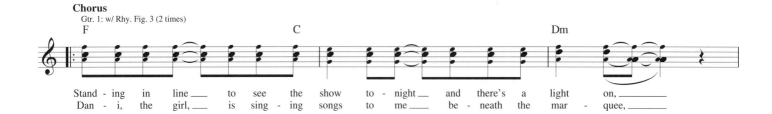

Stand - ing in line ___ to see the show to - night ___ and there's a light on, ___
Dan - i, the girl, ___ is sing - ing songs to me ___ be - neath the mar - quee, ___

heav - y glow. ___ By the way, ___ I tried to say ___ I'd be
o - ver - sold. ___ By the way, ___ I tried to say ___ I know ___

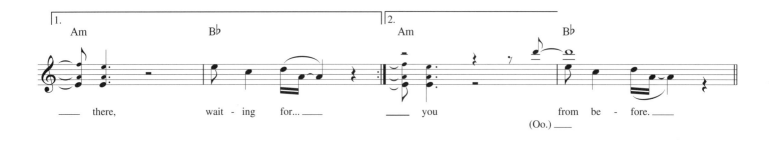

1.
Am   Bb

2.
Am   Bb

___ there,   wait - ing for... ___   ___ you   from be - fore. ___
(Oo.) ___

Outro-Chorus

Gtr. 1: w/ Rhy. Fig. 3 (1st 6 meas.)

Stand - ing in line ___ to see the show to - night ___ and there's a light on, ___

heav - y glow. ___ By the way, ___ I tried to say ___ I'd be ___

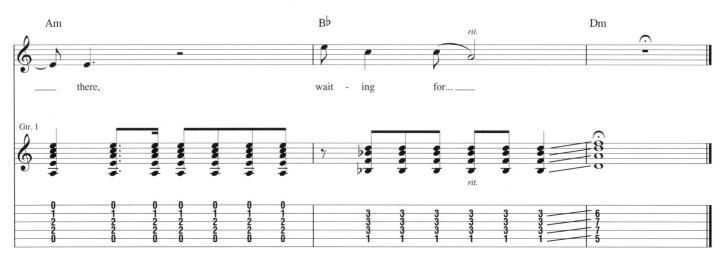

___ there,   wait - ing for... ___

52

Parallel Universe

Words and Music by Anthony Kiedis, Flea, John Frusciante and Chad Smith

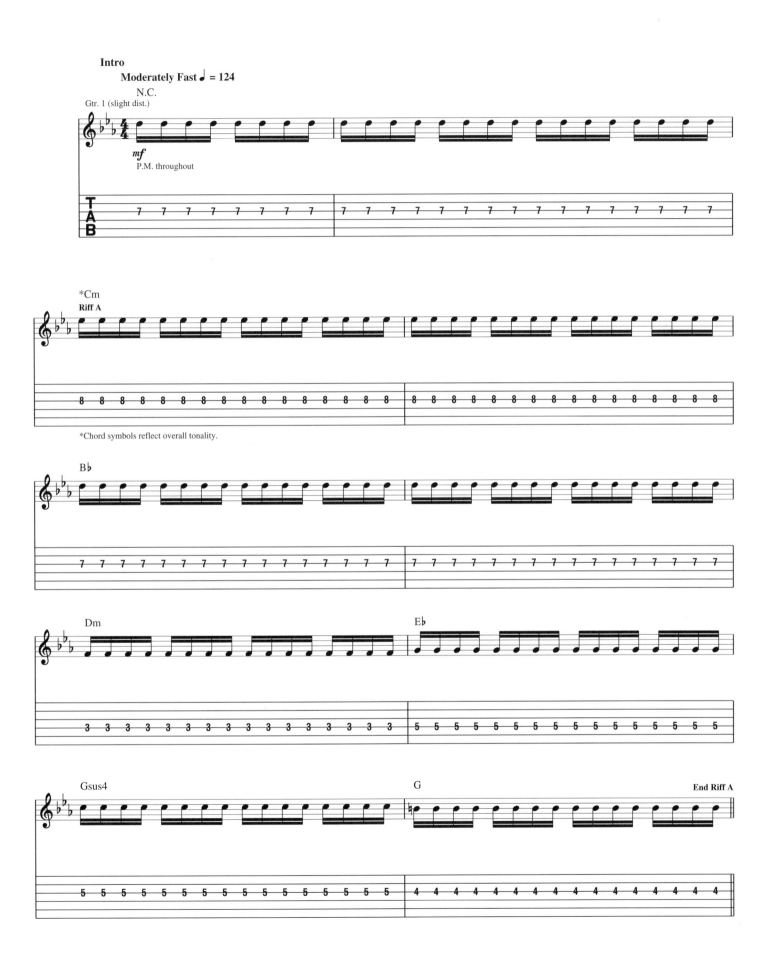

*Chord symbols reflect overall tonality.

Verse

Gtr. 1: w/ Riff A

1. Deep in-side of a par - al-lel u - ni - verse
2. Star-ing straight up in-to the sky, oh, my, my.

it's get-ting hard-er and hard - er to tell what came first,
A so-lar sys-tem that fits in your eye, mi - cro-co - sm.

un - der wa-ter where thoughts can breathe
You could die but you're nev - er dead,

Gtr. 1

*P.M. throughout
simile on repeat

*next 8 meas.

eas - i - ly.
spi - der web.

Far a - way you were made in a sea,
Take a look at the stars in your head,

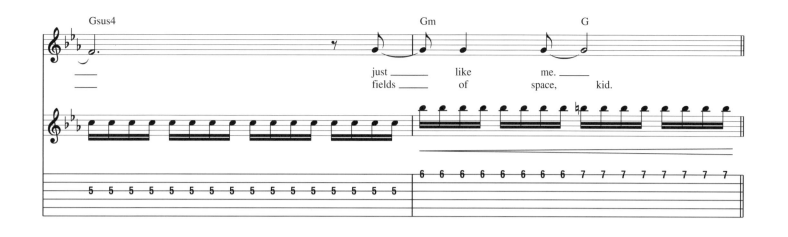

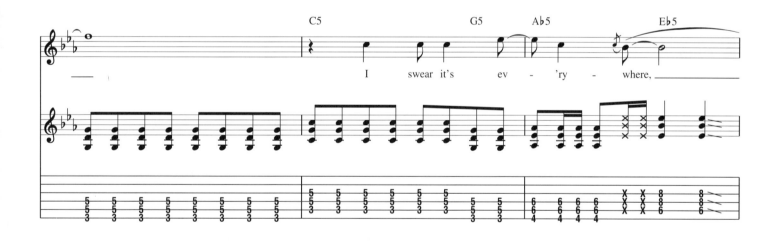

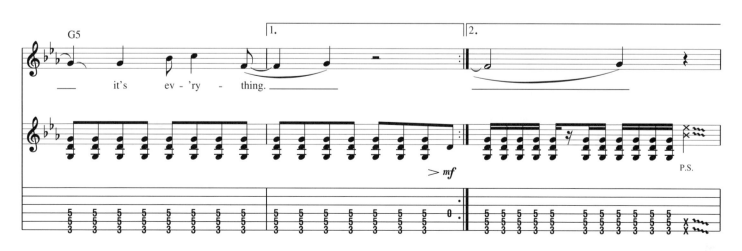

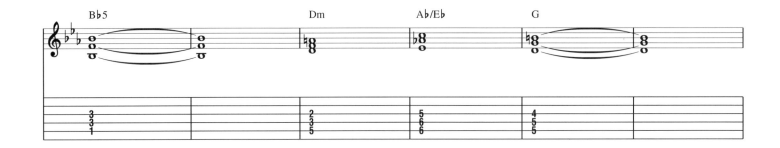

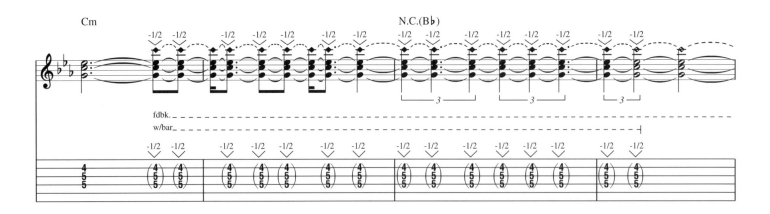

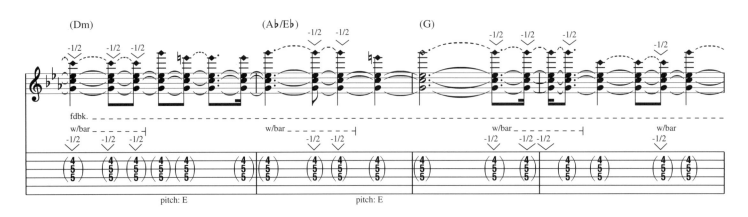

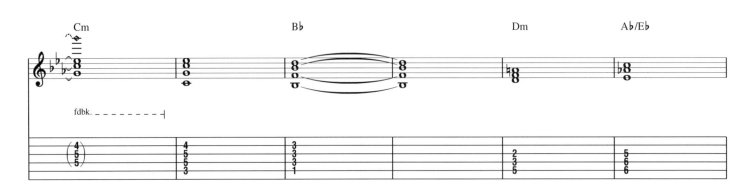

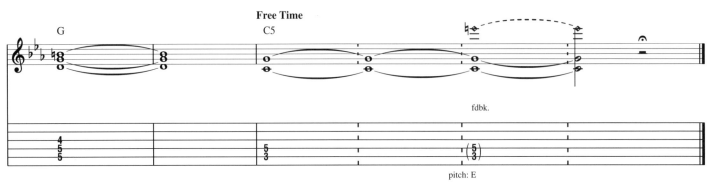

Breaking the Girl

Words and Music by Anthony Kiedis, Flea, John Frusciante and Chad Smith

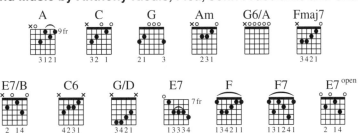

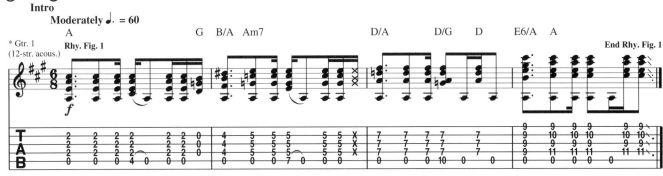

My Friends

Words and Music by Anthony Kiedis, Flea, Chad Smith and David Navarro

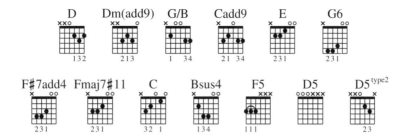

Gtr. 2; Drop D Tuning:
① = E   ④ = D
② = B   ⑤ = A
③ = G   ⑥ = D

Intro
Moderately Slow ♩ = 84

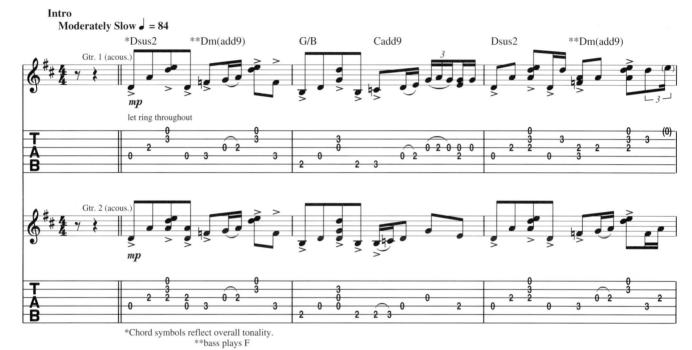

*Chord symbols reflect overall tonality.
**bass plays F

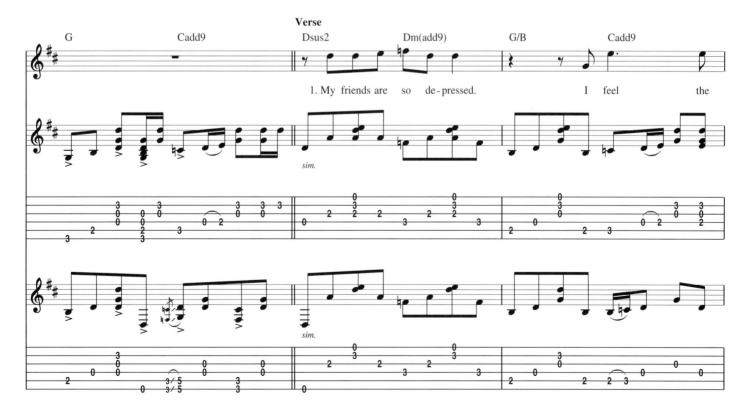

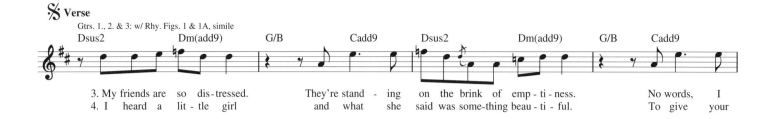

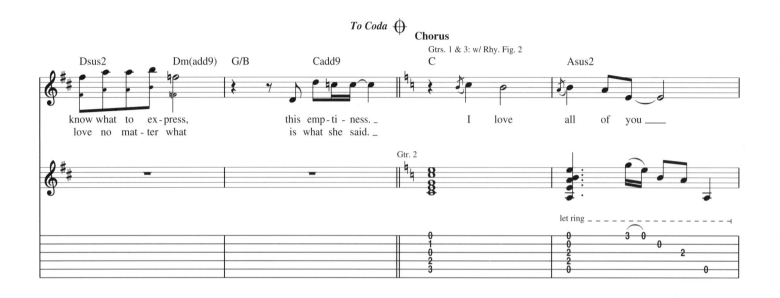

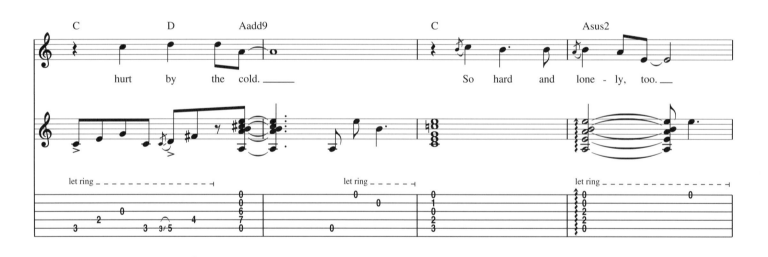

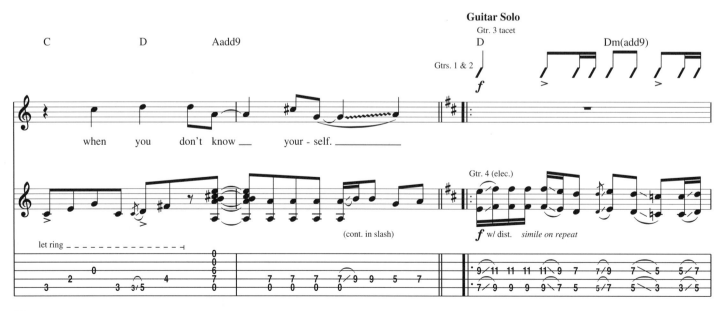

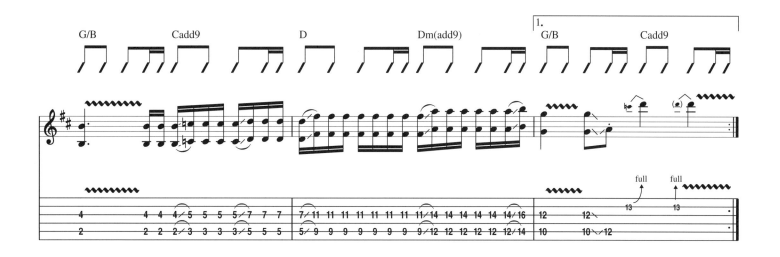

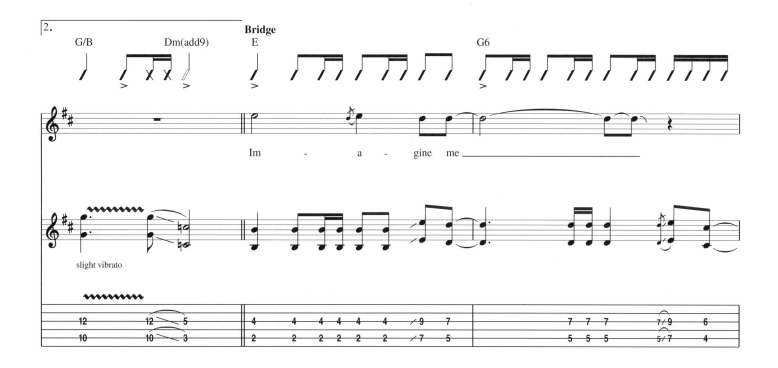

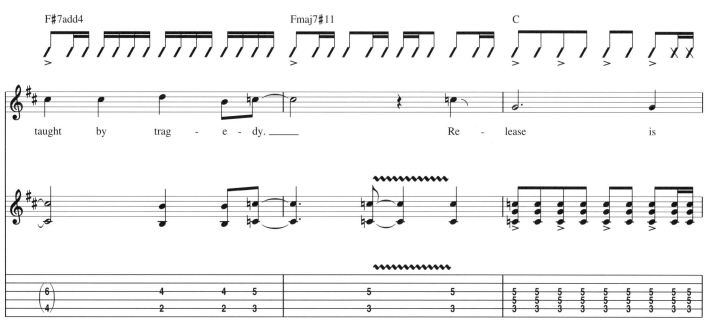

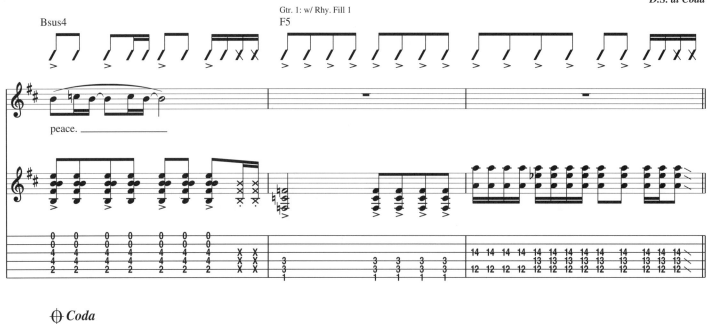

Gtr. 1: w/ Rhy. Fill 1

Bsus4

F5

peace.

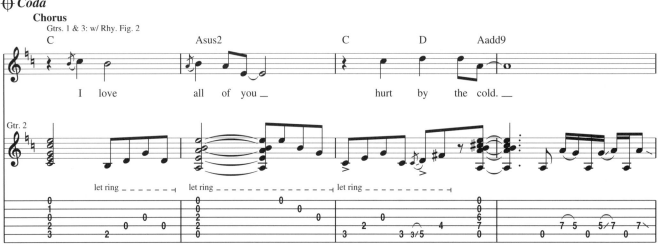

⊕ *Coda*

Chorus

Gtrs. 1 & 3: w/ Rhy. Fig. 2

C   Asus2   C   D   Aadd9

I love   all of you __   hurt by the cold. __

Gtr. 2

let ring _ _ _ _   let ring _ _ _ _ _ _ _   let ring _ _ _ _ _ _ _

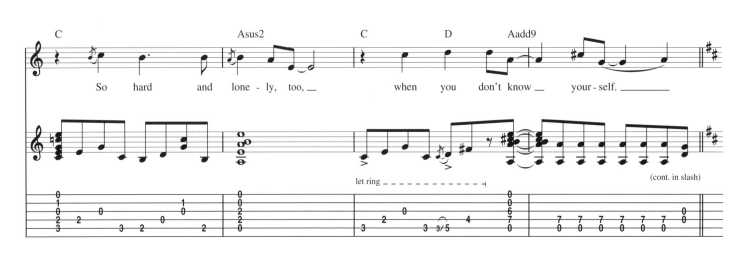

C   Asus2   C   D   Aadd9

So hard and lone - ly, too, __   when you don't know __ your - self. _____

let ring _ _ _ _ _ _ _

(cont. in slash)

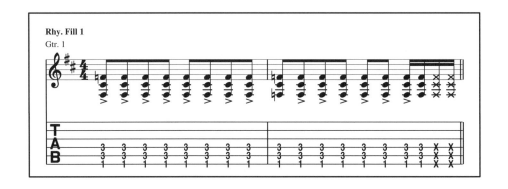

Rhy. Fill 1

Gtr. 1

Outro

Gtr. 3 tacet

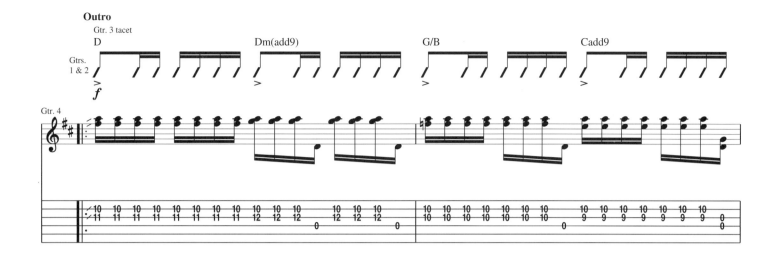

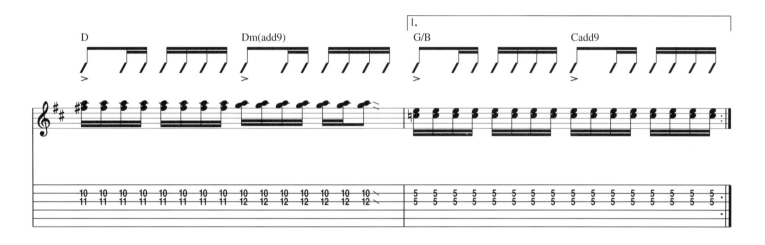

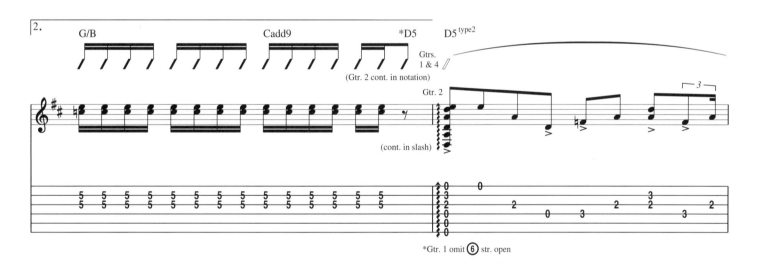

*Gtr. 1 omit ⑥ str. open

Segue to "Coffee Shop"

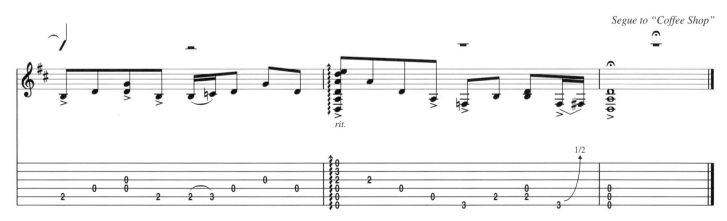

Higher Ground

Words and Music by Stevie Wonder

* Chord symbols reflect basic harmony.

Sol - diers, _____ keep on war - rin'. Uh,

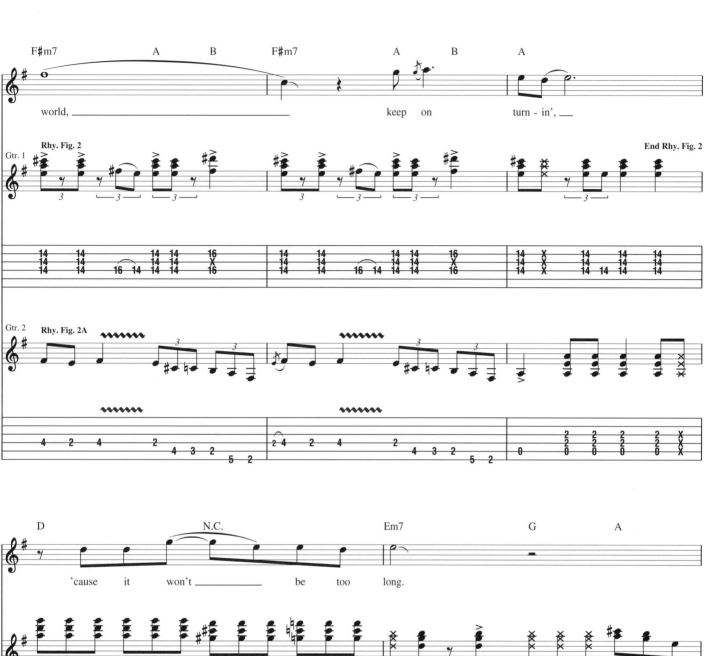

world, _____ keep on turn - in', ___

'cause it won't _____ be too long.

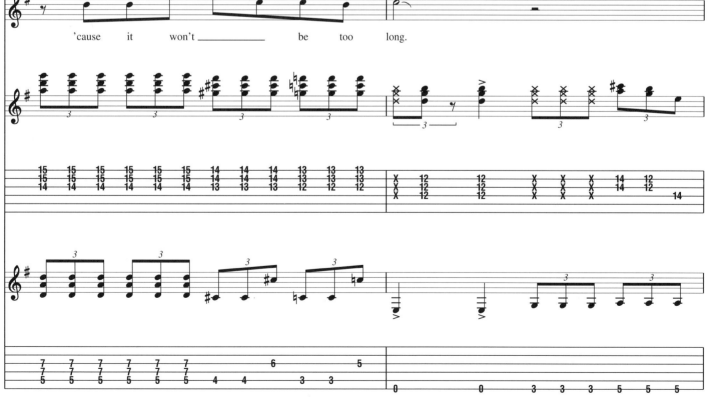

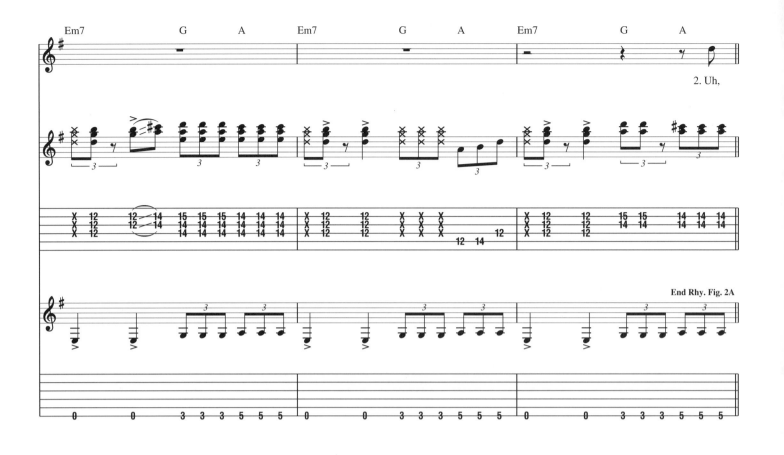

2. Uh,

End Rhy. Fig. 2A

Verse

Gtr. 2: w/ Rhy. Fig. 1 (2 times)
Gtr. 1: w/ Rhy. Fill 1 (4 times)

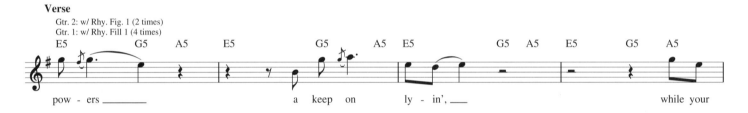

| E5 | G5 A5 | E5 | G5 A5 E5 | G5 A5 E5 | G5 A5 |

pow - ers _____ a keep on ly - in', _____ while your

| E5 | G5 A5 | E5 | G5 A5 E5 | G5 A5 E5 | G5 A5 |

peo - ple _____ a keep on dy - in'. _____ Uh,

Gtrs. 1 & 2: w/ Rhy. Figs. 2 & 2A   Gtr. 1: w/ Rhy. Fill 2

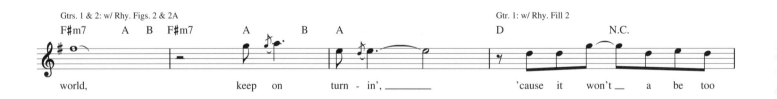

| F#m7 | A B F#m7 | A B A | D | N.C. |

world, keep on turn - in', _____ 'cause it won't _ a be too

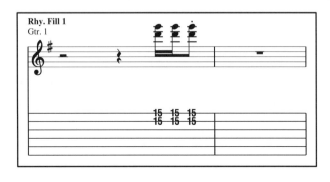

Rhy. Fill 1
Gtr. 1

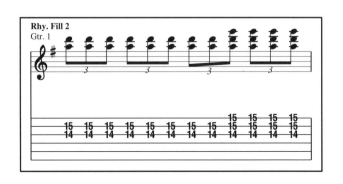

Rhy. Fill 2
Gtr. 1

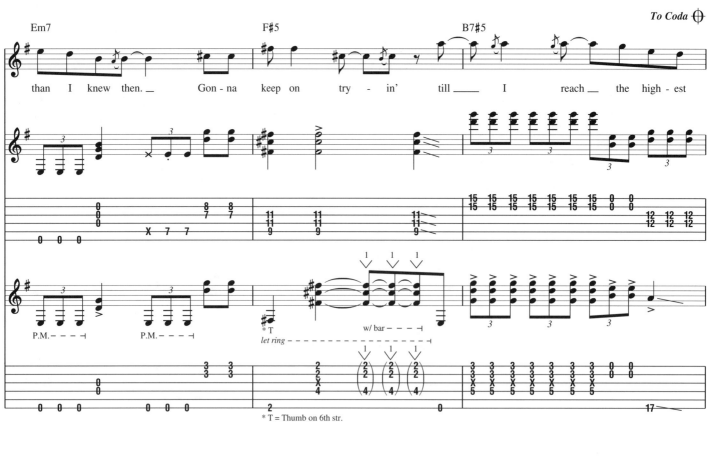

than I knew then. ___ Gon - na keep on try - in' till ___ I reach ___ the high - est

* T = Thumb on 6th str.

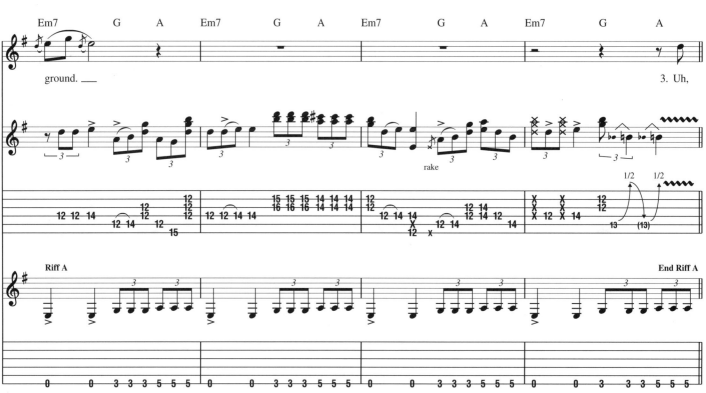

ground. ___   3. Uh,

Riff A   **End Riff A**

Verse

Gtr. 2: w/ Rhy. Fig. 1 (2 times)

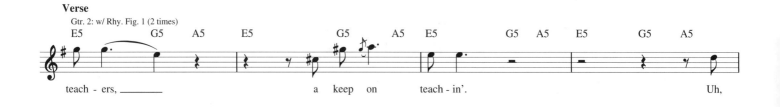

teach - ers, _____   a keep on teach - in'.   Uh,

preach - ers, _____ a keep on preach - in'.

World, _____ keep on turn - in', ____ 'cause it won't _____ be too

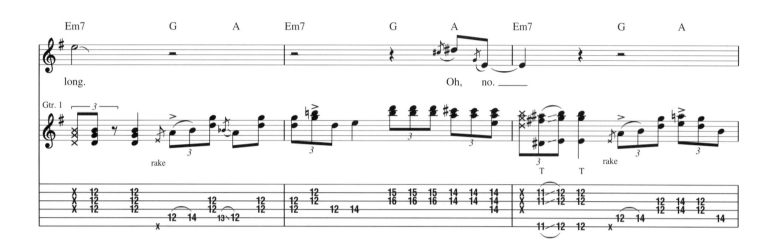

long. Oh, no. _____

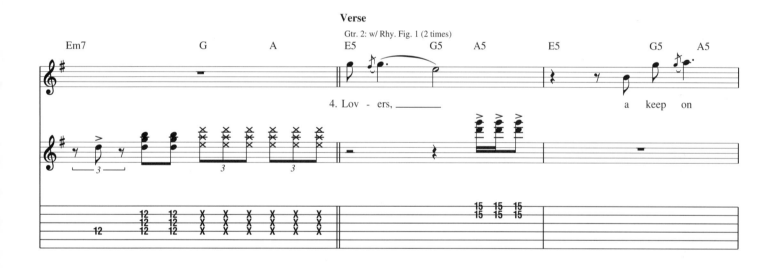

4. Lov - ers, _____ a keep on

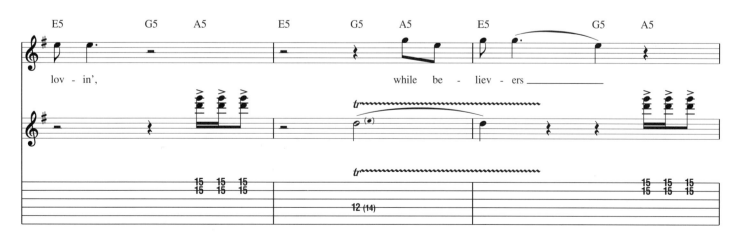

lov - in', while be - liev - ers _____

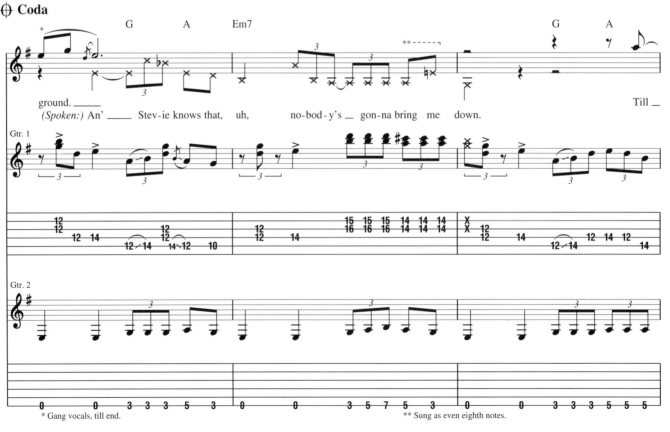

keep on be - liev - in'.

Gtrs. 1 & 2: w/ Rhy. Figs. 2 & 2A

Gtr. 1: w/ Rhy. Fill 2

Sleep - ers, ___ just stop sleep - in', ___ 'cause it won't ___ be too

Gtr. 2: w/ Riff A

D.S. al Coda

long. Oh, no! ___ I'm

Gtr. 1

⊕ **Coda**

ground. ___

(Spoken:) An' ___ Stev-ie knows that, uh, no-bod-y's ___ gon-na bring me down.

Till ___

Gtr. 1

Gtr. 2

* Gang vocals, till end.

** Sung as even eighth notes.

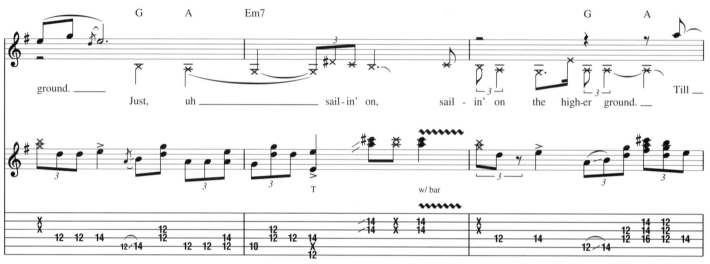

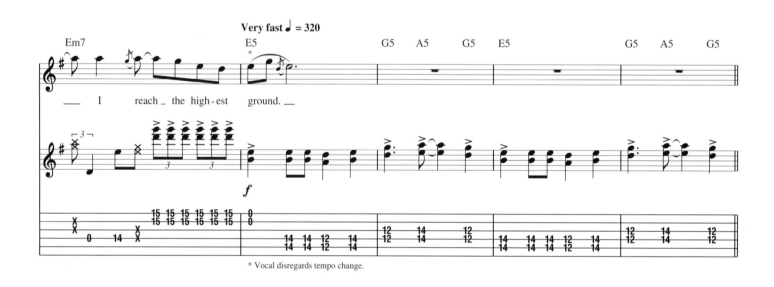

* Vocal disregards tempo change.

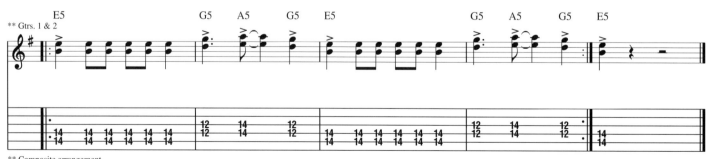

** Composite arrangement.

Universally Speaking

Words and Music by Anthony Kiedis, Flea, John Frusciante and Chad Smith

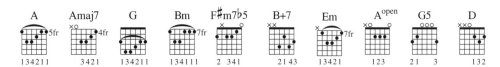

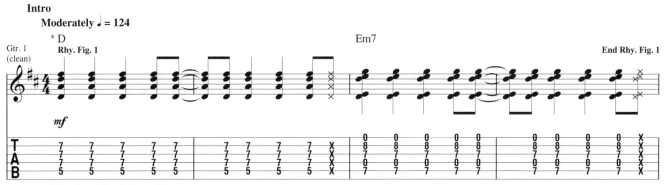

Intro

Moderately ♩ = 124

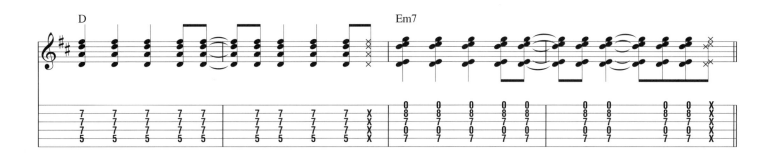

* Chord symbols reflect overall harmony.

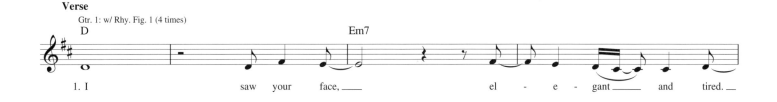

Verse

Gtr. 1: w/ Rhy. Fig. 1 (4 times)

1. I saw your face, ____ el - e - gant ____ and tired. ____

____ Cut up from the chase, ___ still ___ I so ___ ad - mired. ___

____ Blood - shot, your smile, ___ del - i - cate ___ and wild. ___

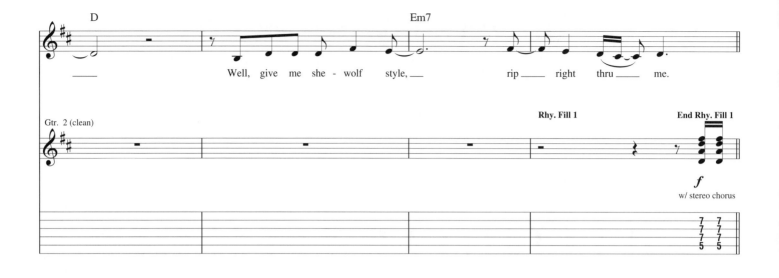

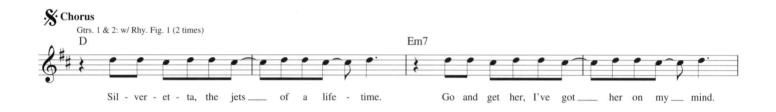

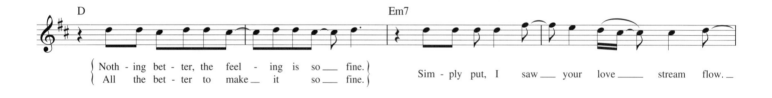

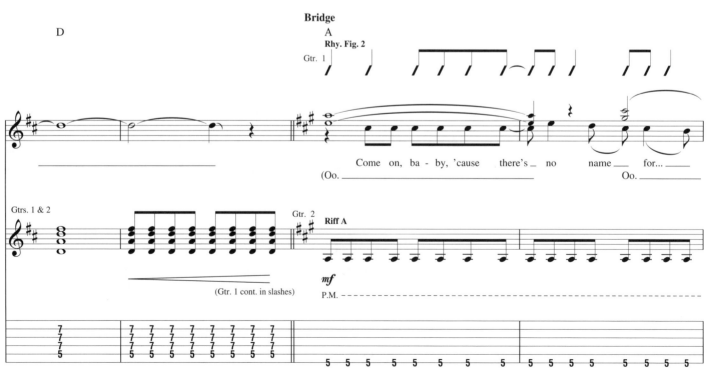

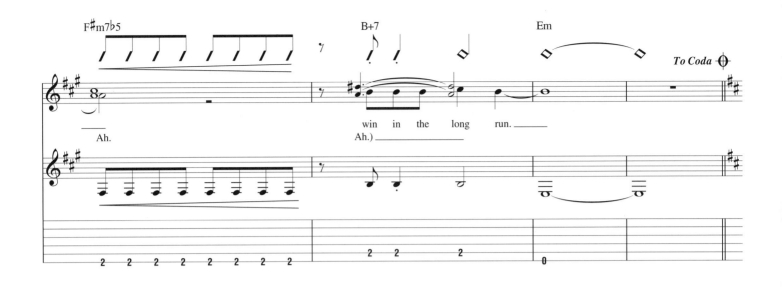

Interlude

Gtr. 1: w/ Rhy. Fig. 1 (2 times)
Gtr. 2 tacet

Verse

Gtr. 1: w/ Rhy. Fig. 1 (2 times)

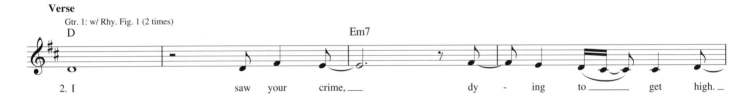

2. I saw your crime, dy-ing to get high.

D.S. al Coda

Gtr. 2: w/ Rhy. Fill 1

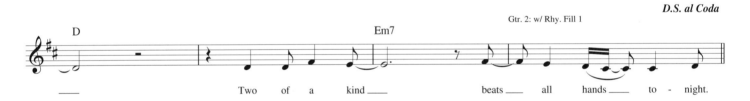

Two of a kind beats all hands to-night.

Coda

Chorus

Gtr. 1: w/ Rhy. Fig. 1 (3 times)
Gtr. 2 tacet

Sil-ver-et-ta, the jets of a life-time. Go and get her, I've got her on my mind.

Noth-ing bet-ter, the feel-ing is so fine. Sim-ply put, I saw your love stream flow.

Sim-ply put, I saw your love stream flow.

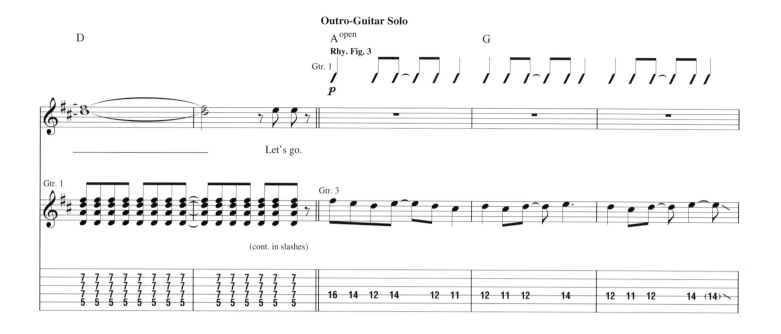

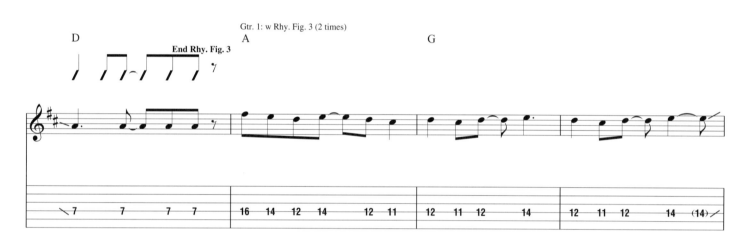

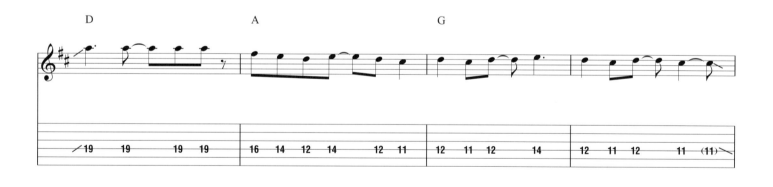

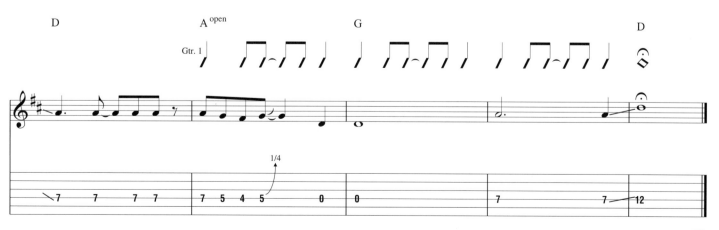

Road Trippin'

Words and Music by Anthony Kiedis, Flea, John Frusciante and Chad Smith

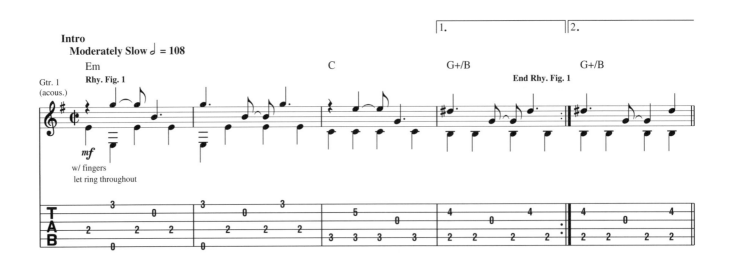

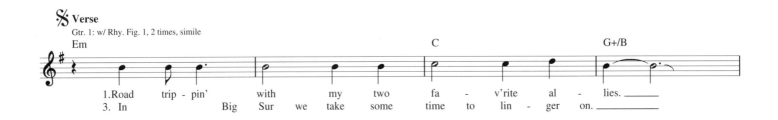

Road trip-pin' with my two fa-v'rite al - lies. _____
In Big Sur we take some time to lin - ger on. _____

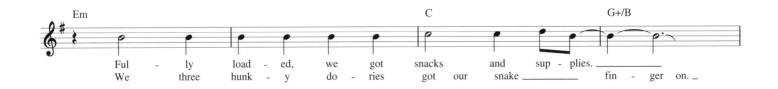

Ful - ly load - ed, we got snacks and sup - plies. _____
We three hunk - y do - ries got our snake _____ fin - ger on. _

It's time to leave _____ this town, it's time to steal a - way. _____
Now let us drink the stars, it's time to steal a - way. _____

Gtr. 1: w/ Rhy. Fig. 1

Em   C   G+/B

Let's __ go get lost __ an-y-where in the U. S. A. __
Let's __ go get lost __ right here in the U. S. A. __

Gtr. 1: w/ Rhy. Fig. 2

Chorus
Gtr. 1: w/ Rhy. Fig. 1, 4 times, simile

Em   C   G+/B   Em

Let's go get lost, __ let's go get lost. __   Blue, you

C   G+/B   Em

sit so pret-ty west of the one. _____ Spar-kles light with yel-low

C   G+/B   Em   C

ic-ing, just a mir-ror for the sun.   Just a

G+/B   Em   C   G+/B

mir-ror for __ the sun. __   Just a mir-ror for the

To Coda ⊕

Am   G/B   C   *G/D

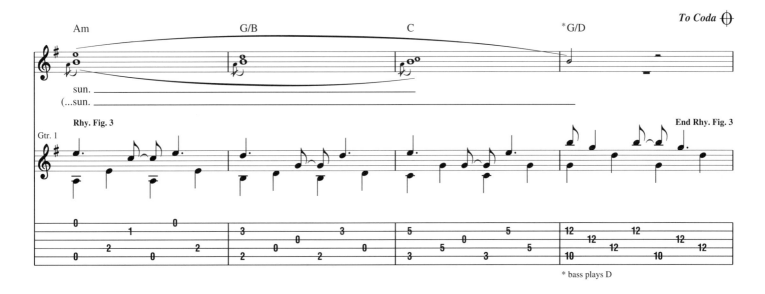

sun. _____
(...sun. _____)

Rhy. Fig. 3   End Rhy. Fig. 3

Gtr. 1

* bass plays D

Verse
Gtr. 1: w/ Rhy. Fig. 1, 2 times, simile

Gtr. 1: w/ Rhy. Fig. 3

Am   G/B   C   G/D   Em

These smil-ing eyes __ are just a mir-ror for... __   2. So much as
Mir - ror for. _____)

C G+/B Em
came be - fore __ those bat - tles lost and won. This life is shin - ing more for -
Chorus
Gtr. 1: w/ Rhy. Fig. 2
C G+/B Em C
ev - er in the sun. __ Now let us check __ our heads __ and let us check the surf. __
Gtr. 1: w/ Rhy. Fig. 1, 3 times
G+/B Em C G+/B
__ Stay - ing high and dry's more trou - ble than it's worth in the sun. __
Em C G+/B Em
__ Just a mir - ror for __ the sun. __
Gtr. 1: w/ Rhy. Fig. 3, 2 times
C G+/B Am G/B C
Just a mir - ror for the sun. __
(...sun. __
G/D Am G/B C G/D
These smil - ing eyes __ are just a mir - ror for... __
__ Mir - ror for. __)
Interlude
Em7 A7 C D7
Gtr. 1
simile on repeat
Em7 A7 C D#°7/F#
1.

D.S. al Coda

* Barre highest 4 strings w/ L.H. index finger.

⊕ Coda

Gtr. 1: w/ Rhy. Fig. 3, 3 times

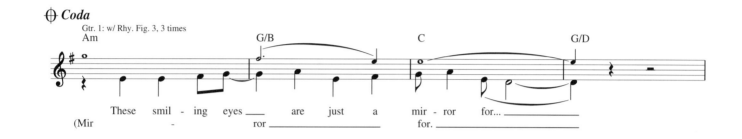

These smil-ing eyes ___ are just a mir-ror for... ___
(Mir - ror ___ for. ___

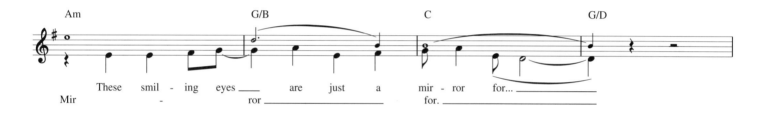

These smil-ing eyes ___ are just a mir-ror for... ___
Mir - ror ___ for. ___

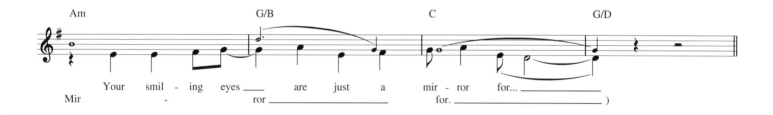

Your smil-ing eyes ___ are just a mir-ror for... ___
Mir - ror ___ for. ___)

Outro

Gtr. 1

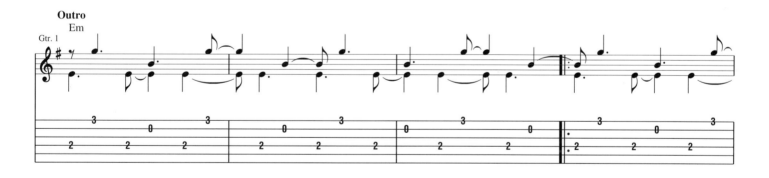

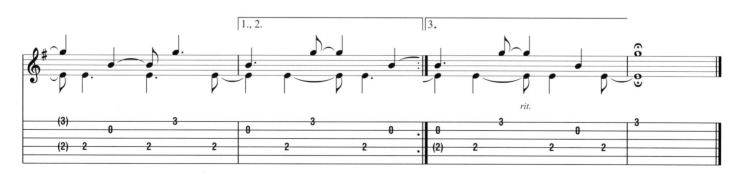

rit.

Fortune Faded

Words and Music by Anthony Kiedis, Flea, John Frusciante and Chad Smith

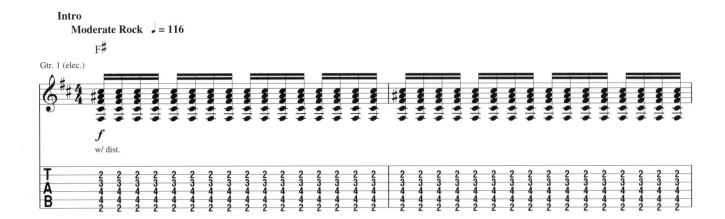

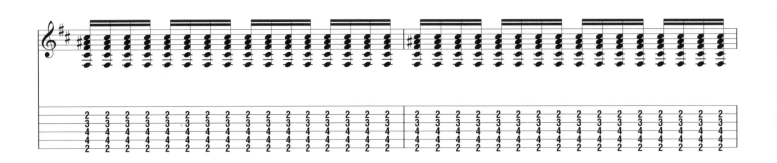

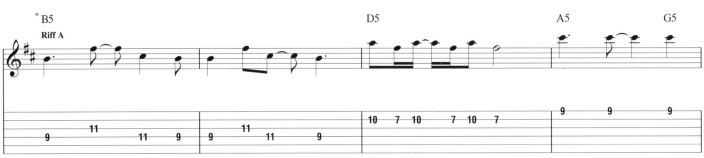

*Chord symbols reflect implied harmony.

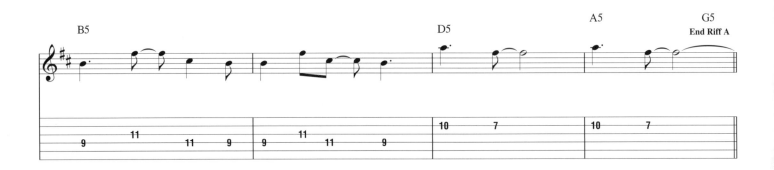

1. They say in chess ____ you've got to kill ____ the queen and then you made it, ____
2. You took a town ____ by storm, the mess you made was nom - i - nat - ed, ____
3. The med - i - cat - ed state of mind ____ you found is o - ver - rat - ed, ____

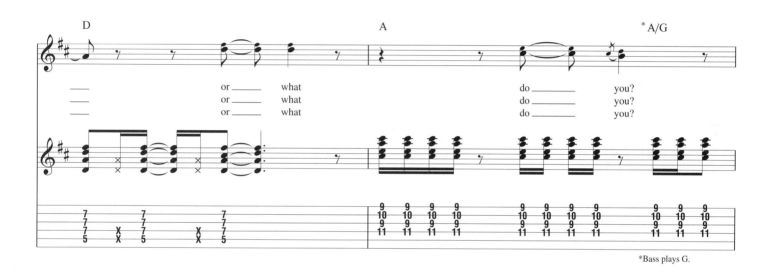

____ or ____ what   do ____ you?
____ or ____ what   do ____ you?
____ or ____ what   do ____ you?

*Bass plays G.

A   fun - ny   thing, ____   the   king   who   gets   him - self   as - sas - si - nat - ed. ____
Now put a - way ____   your wel - come, soon you find you've o - ver - stayed it. ____
You saw it all ____   come down and now it's time to im - i - tate it. ____

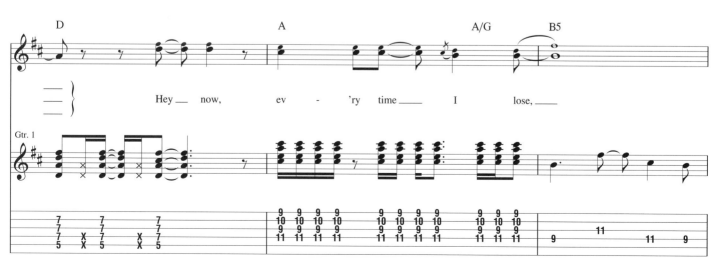

Hey ____ now,   ev - 'ry time ____   I   lose, ____

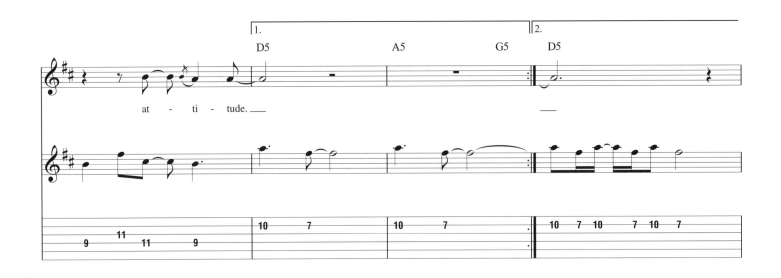

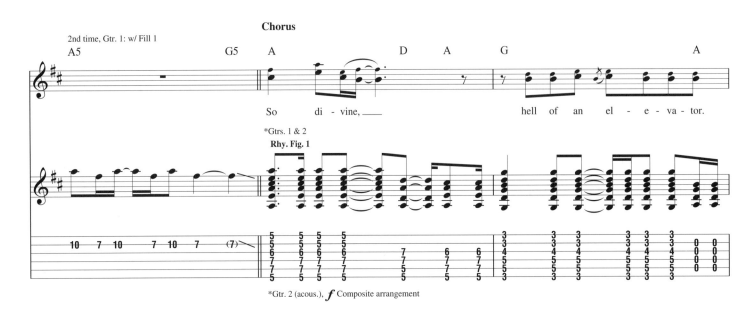

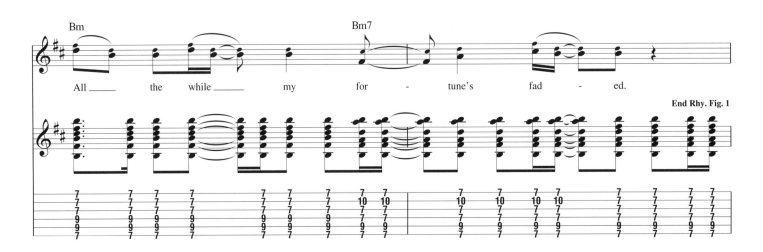

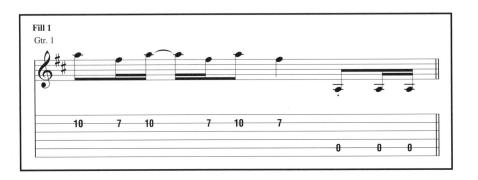

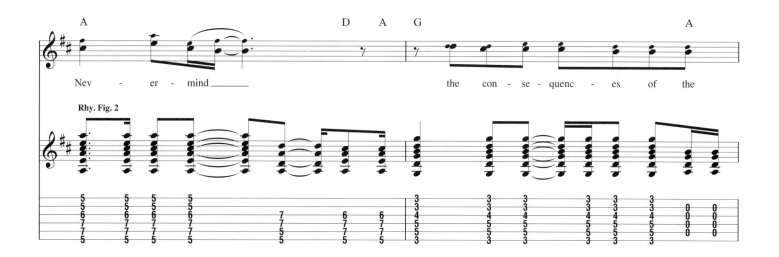

To Coda ⊕

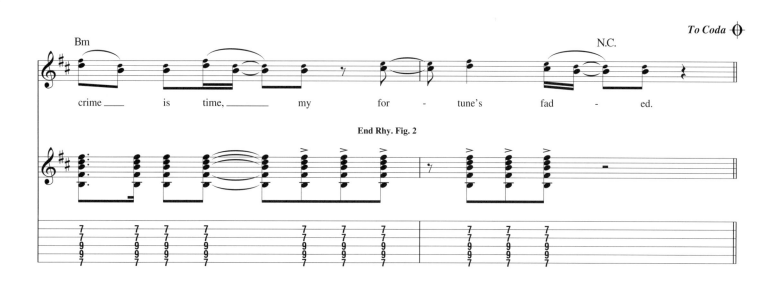

D.S. al Coda
(take 2nd ending)

Interlude
Gtr. 1: w/ Riff A
Gtr. 2 tacet

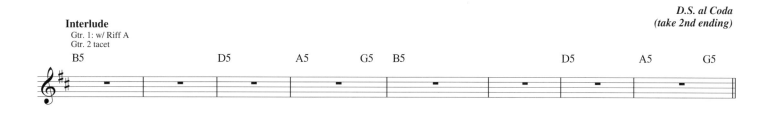

⊕ **Coda**

Bridge
Gtrs. 1 & 2 tacet

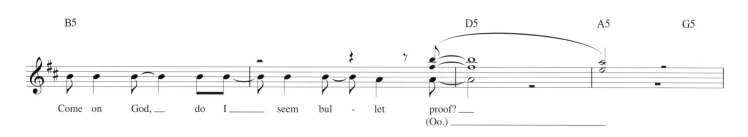

Gtr. 1
F#

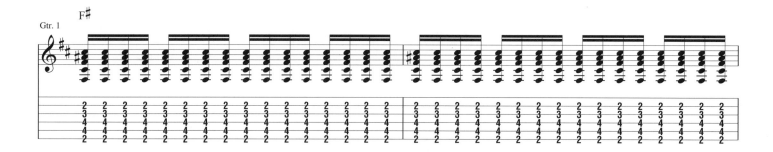

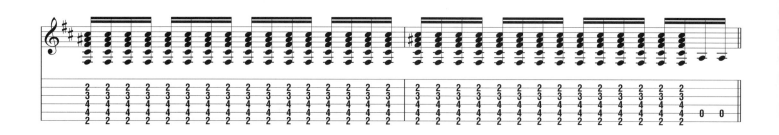

Chorus
Gtrs. 1 & 2: w/ Rhy. Fig. 1 (3 times)

So di - vine, _____ hell of an el - e - va - tor. All _____ the while _____ my for -

- tune's fad - ed. Nev - er - mind _____ the con - se - quenc - es of the crime _ is time, _____ my for -

- tune's _____ fad - ed. So di - vine, _____ hell of an el - e - va - tor.

Gtrs. 1 & 2: w/ Rhy. Fig. 2

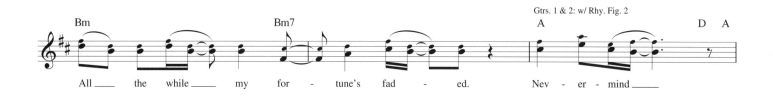

All _____ the while _____ my for - tune's fad - ed. Nev - er - mind _____

the con - se - quenc - es of the crime _ is time, _____ my for - tune's fad - ed.

Save the Population

Words and Music by Anthony Kiedis, Flea, John Frusciante and Chad Smith

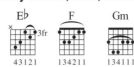

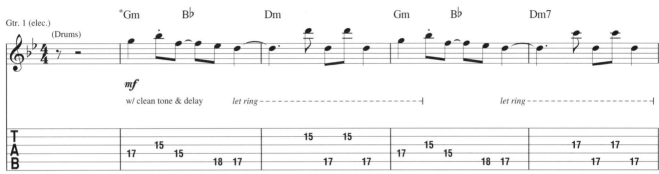

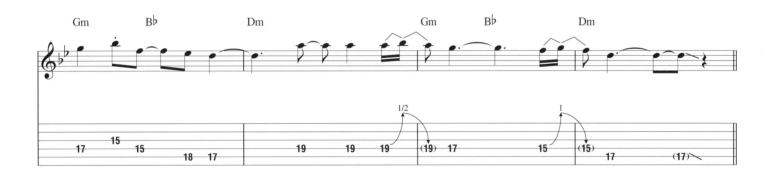

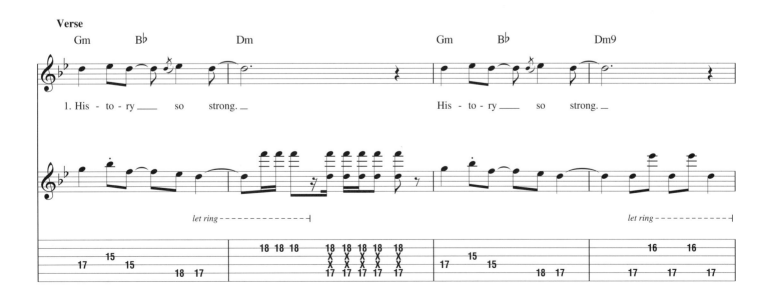

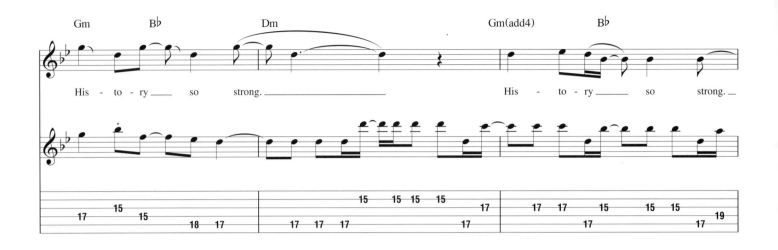

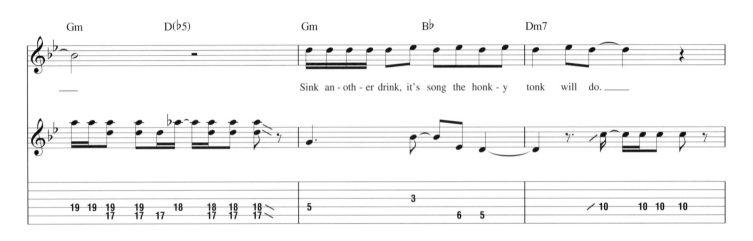

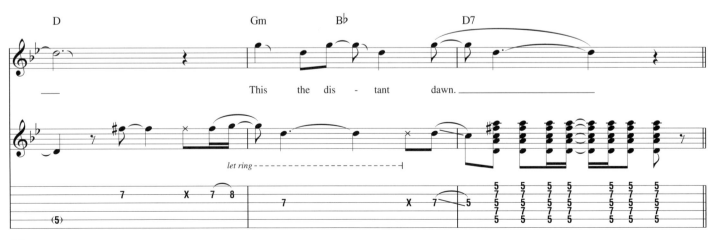

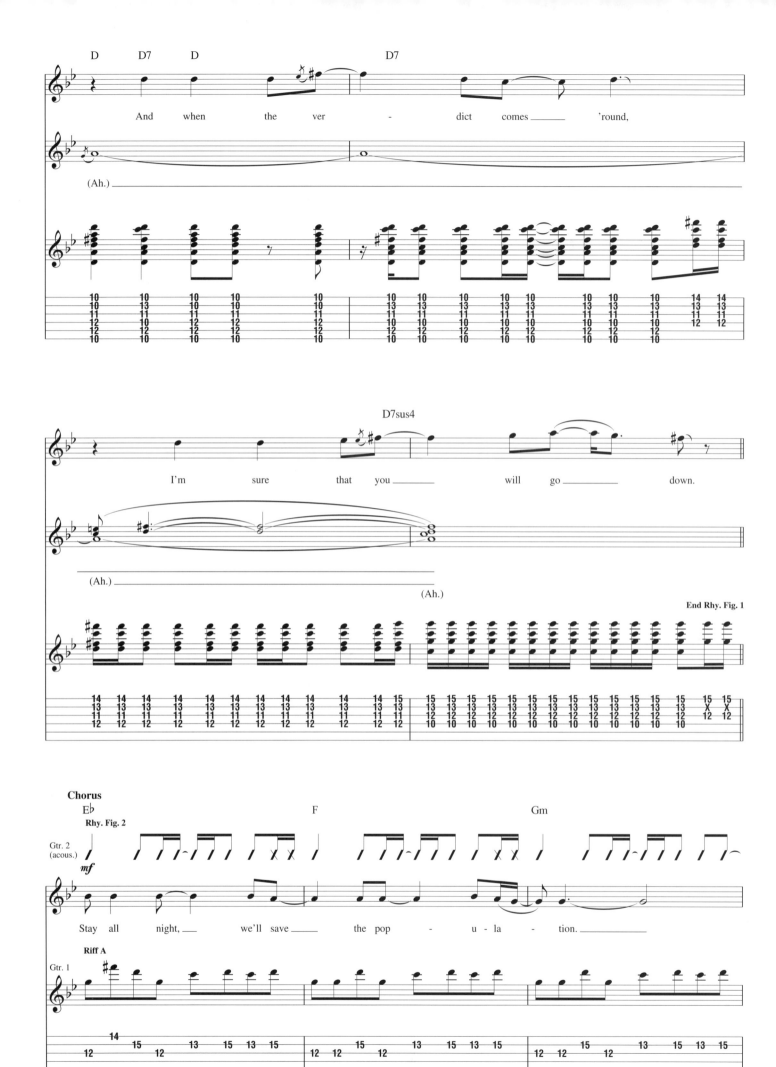

Interlude

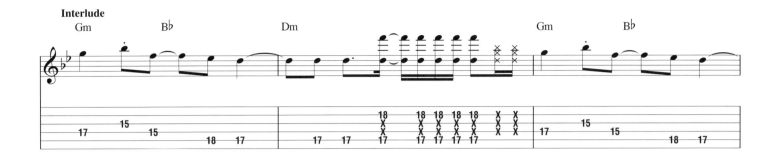

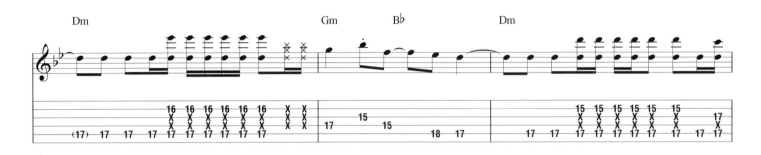

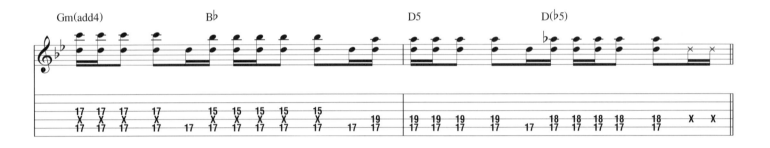

Verse

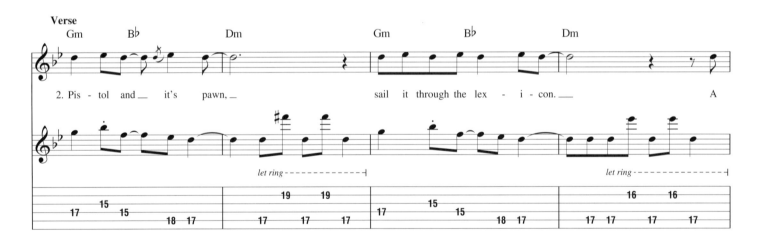

2. Pis - tol and __ it's pawn, __ sail it through the lex - i - con. __ A

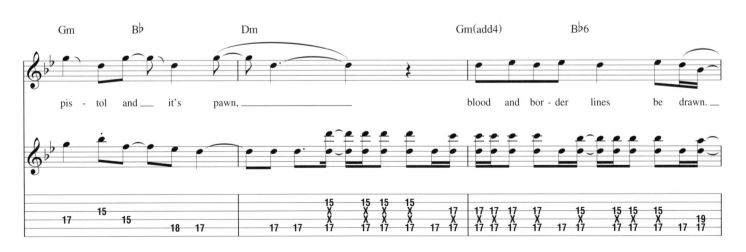

pis - tol and __ it's pawn, _____ blood and bor - der lines be drawn. __

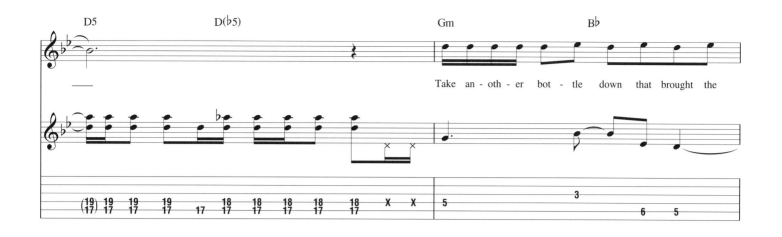

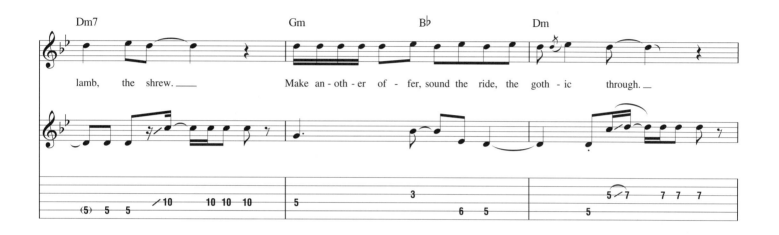

Pre-Chorus

Gtr. 1: w/ Rhy. Fig. 1

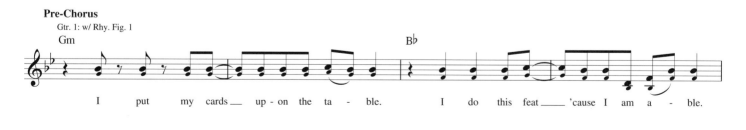

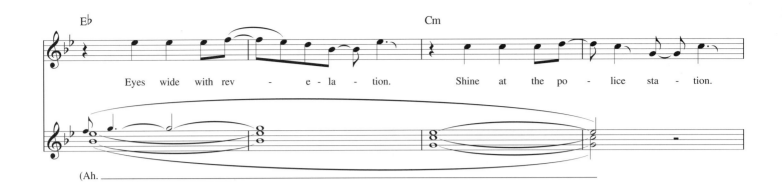

Eyes wide with rev - e - la - tion. Shine at the po - lice sta - tion.

(Ah.

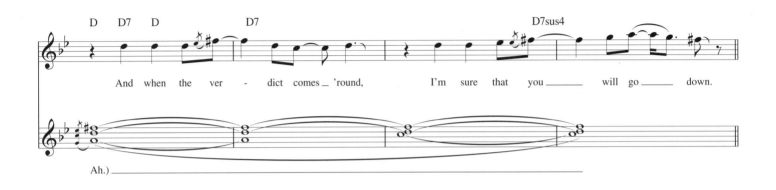

And when the ver - dict comes __ 'round, I'm sure that you ___ will go ___ down.

Ah.)

Chorus

Gtr. 1: w/ Riff A (5 1/2 times)
Gtr. 2: w/ Rhy. Fig. 2 (5 1/2 times)

Stay all night, __ we'll save ___ the pop - u - la - tion. ___

Stay all night, __ we'll save ___ the pop - u - la -

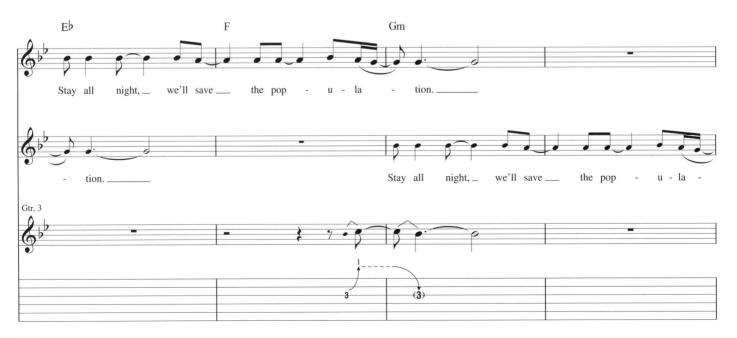

Stay all night, __ we'll save ___ the pop - u - la - tion. ___

- tion. ___ Stay all night, __ we'll save ___ the pop - u - la -

Gtr. 3

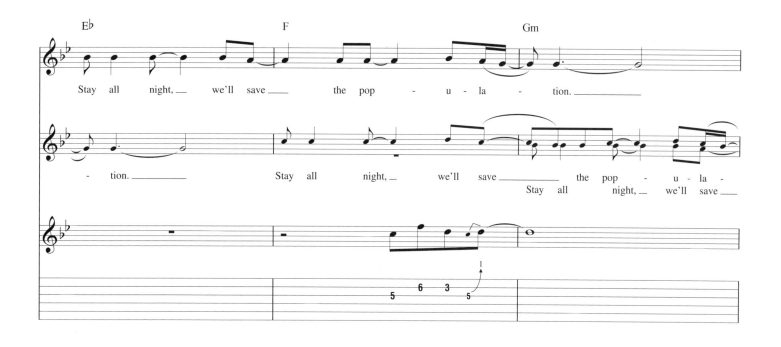

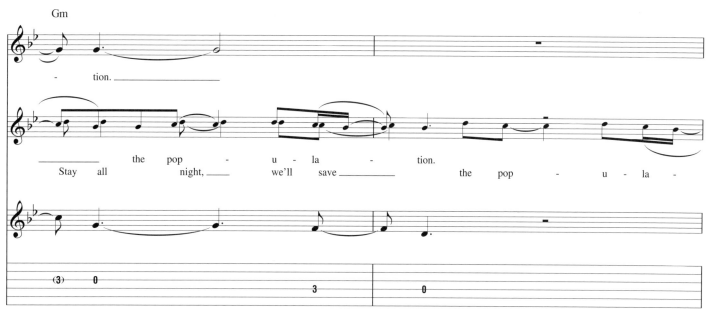

Stay all night, __ we'll save ____ the pop - u - la - tion. _____

- tion. Stay all night, __ we'll save ____ the pop - u - la -
Stay all night, __ we'll save ____

Stay all night, __ we'll save ____ the pop - u - la -

- tion. Stay all night, __ we'll save ____
_____ the pop - u - la - tion.

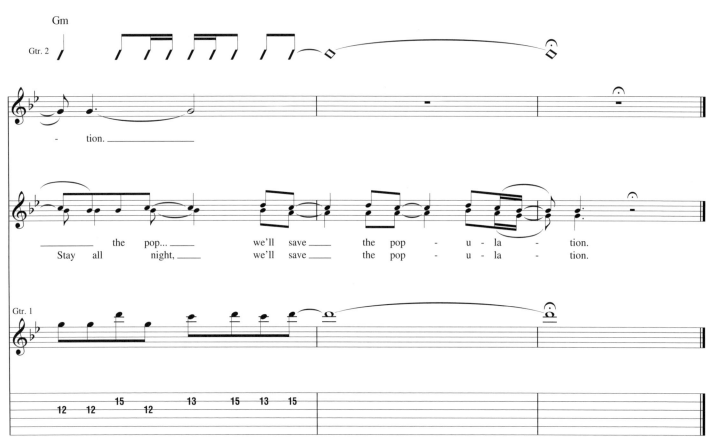

- tion. _____

_____ the pop... _____ we'll save ____ the pop - u - la - tion.
Stay all night, _____ we'll save ____ the pop - u - la - tion.

Guitar Notation Legend

Guitar Music can be notated three different ways: on a *musical staff*, in *tablature*, and in *rhythm slashes*.

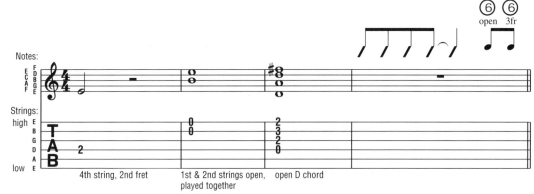

RHYTHM SLASHES are written above the staff. Strum chords in the rhythm indicated. Use the chord diagrams found at the top of the first page of the transcription for the appropriate chord voicings. Round noteheads indicate single notes.

THE MUSICAL STAFF shows pitches and rhythms and is divided by bar lines into measures. Pitches are named after the first seven letters of the alphabet.

TABLATURE graphically represents the guitar fingerboard. Each horizontal line represents a string, and each number represents a fret.

HALF-STEP BEND: Strike the note and bend up 1/2 step.

WHOLE-STEP BEND: Strike the note and bend up one step.

GRACE NOTE BEND: Strike the note and immediately bend up as indicated.

SLIGHT (MICROTONE) BEND: Strike the note and bend up 1/4 step.

BEND AND RELEASE: Strike the note and bend up as indicated, then release back to the original note. Only the first note is struck.

PRE-BEND: Bend the note as indicated, then strike it.

VIBRATO: The string is vibrated by rapidly bending and releasing the note with the fretting hand.

WIDE VIBRATO: The pitch is varied to a greater degree by vibrating with the fretting hand.

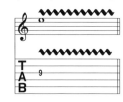

HAMMER-ON: Strike the first (lower) note with one finger, then sound the higher note (on the same string) with another finger by fretting it without picking.

PULL-OFF: Place both fingers on the notes to be sounded. Strike the first note and without picking, pull the finger off to sound the second (lower) note.

LEGATO SLIDE: Strike the first note and then slide the same fret-hand finger up or down to the second note. The second note is not struck.

SHIFT SLIDE: Same as legato slide, except the second note is struck.

TRILL: Very rapidly alternate between the notes indicated by continuously hammering on and pulling off.

TAPPING: Hammer ("tap") the fret indicated with the pick-hand index or middle finger and pull off to the note fretted by the fret hand.

NATURAL HARMONIC: Strike the note while the fret-hand lightly touches the string directly over the fret indicated.

PINCH HARMONIC: The note is fretted normally and a harmonic is produced by adding the edge of the thumb or the tip of the index finger of the pick hand to the normal pick attack.

PICK SCRAPE: The edge of the pick is rubbed down (or up) the string, producing a scratchy sound.

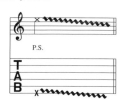

MUFFLED STRINGS: A percussive sound is produced by laying the fret hand across the string(s) without depressing, and striking them with the pick hand.

PALM MUTING: The note is partially muted by the pick hand lightly touching the string(s) just before the bridge.

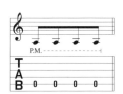

RAKE: Drag the pick across the strings indicated with a single motion.

TREMOLO PICKING: The note is picked as rapidly and continuously as possible.

VIBRATO BAR DIVE AND RETURN: The pitch of the note or chord is dropped a specified number of steps (in rhythm) then returned to the original pitch.

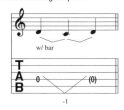

VIBRATO BAR SCOOP: Depress the bar just before striking the note, then quickly release the bar.

VIBRATO BAR DIP: Strike the note and then immediately drop a specified number of steps, then release back to the original pitch.

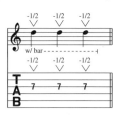

RECORDED VERSIONS
The Best Note-For-Note Transcriptions Available

ALL BOOKS INCLUDE TABLATURE